BUD LILLY AND PAUL SCHULLERY

A TROUT'S BEST FRIEND

THE ANGLING AUTOBIOGRAPHY OF BUD LILLY

BUD LILLY AND PAUL SCHULLERY

A TROUT'S BEST FRIEND

THE ANGLING AUTOBIOGRAPHY OF BUD LILLY

PRUETT **P** PUBLISHING COMPANY
Boulder, Colorado

Printed in the United States of America

First Edition
1 2 3 4 5 6 7 8 9

Library of Congress Cataloging-in-Publication Data

Lilly, Bud.
  A trout's best friend.

  1. Fishing—Montana.   2. Trout fishing—Montana.
3. Fly fishing—Montana.   I. Schullery, Paul.
II. Title.
SH517.L55   1988   799.1′755   88-9766
ISBN 0-87108-745-6
ISBN 0-87108-744-8 (pbk.)

To my former customers, fishing friends, and family who helped make all this fun happen.

MONTANA BEGINNINGS

7

FIVE DOLLARS AND A CLEAN SHIRT

27

A FLYFISHING FAMILY

53

CLIENTS AND OTHER CHALLENGES

67

EXPERTS

87

A TROUT'S BEST FRIEND

115

ONCE A GUIDE

137

Bud Lilly and fly fishing were total strangers to me when I began a major assignment to explore the marvels and the issues of Yellowstone country. We rendezvoused in the Park just after the Yellowstone River season opened in mid-July, near the mouth of Otter Creek, a little above the upper falls of the Grand Canyon.

For two days I watched Bud's eyes scan the stream, picking out cutthroat rise from river riffle, and then, precisely, softly presenting his wooly worm or dry fly with long, clean loops of line. Those were raw, gray days on the river; Lilly made them warm with his patient efforts to demystify the art. As we fished, I learned of Bud's ancestors pioneering into the Gallatin Valley, and of his participation in the campaign that transformed the Park's waters from a worn-out meat fishery into a sportsman's dream. It was easy to become a friend and admirer of Bud Lilly in two days. Fly fishing will take a little longer, as it should.

SY FISHBEIN
Retired Editor/Writer,
Special Publications Division,
National Geographic Society

I had a customer who had been a friend for many years. Horace had started coming to West Yellowstone in the 1930s, and by the 1950s he was in very poor health. His hearing was shot, he had to carry a little oxygen bottle with him, and he could just barely see. He still wanted to fish, though, and so he showed up as usual one summer for some guided trips. We had taken him the year before in a boat, though that hadn't worked out well because it rained on the poor guy all day. The limitations of his health were catching up with him to the point that there was hardly any fishing he could still do.

So Horace asked if I could take him personally. I agreed and said, "Let's go down on the Madison. The salmonflies are on."

"Oh, God, I can't handle that anymore, Bud."

"All right," I said. "I know a man who might let us get in and fish Odell Creek above Ennis." So we went down, and my friend, having some sympathy for Horace, let us fish. It was quite a production getting him out to the creek, what with his oxygen bottle and all, but we managed it, though I could tell he was pretty tired by the time we got there.

Luckily the salmonflies were hatching on the main river nearby, and some of them were flying over and laying their eggs in the creek. As I was leading Horace along, I watched the creek and saw a huge boil as a big trout took a fly. Trying to sound calm about it, I said, "I think I got one spotted, Horace." I tied on a Sofa Pillow, and he picked up his oxygen bottle and off we went. I could see a fish sloshing around, and could tell it was very large.

I got him into position. "Horace, he's about in there, just off that bank."

"Huh? What was that?"

"*He's over that way!*"

"Oh. Okay."

After a little fumbling and a lot of coaching, he did manage to get a cast to within about three feet of the fish, which generously rushed the fly and took it. I yelled, "He's got it!"

"Whatsat?" Horace asked, as the fish hooked himself.

Now Horace, being an experienced fisherman, knew what to do once he had a fish on the line. So it wasn't long before the fish was in, and I got it close enough for him to admire. It was a gorgeous brown trout.

"How big is he?"

"Oh, I'd say he's about twenty-one inches, probably three or four pounds."

"What fly was that I was using?"

"A Sofa Pillow."

"What tippet?"

"4X, Horace." In that little creek, with its clear water, I had to put on a pretty fine tippet even for the large fly.

"Let me see the leader." I handed him the leader, which he started coiling up, so I asked, "What are you going to do?"

"That's it. I'm quitting."

"Quitting? Hell, that's the first fish of the day. There are lots more big fish in here."

"That's right, but that's as fine a fish as I've ever caught, and that's the last one I'll ever catch. Let's go home."

That, whatever else I may tell you about in this book, was my most memorable fish. That man had caught fish for forty years, and he dearly loved the sport, but he had the wisdom to recognize his last trout when it came along. No fishing memory I have will ever equal that one; no trout I catch will ever mean that much to me.

Fly fishing for trout has been an important part of my life for more than fifty years. I have no idea how many trout I've caught, though I do know that back in my early days I killed many more than I should have. There's no point in apologizing for that because at the time, it was just something people did. You caught a fish, you killed it. But those early days did teach me that it isn't the killing that you remember best. It's everything that goes into the day, from the companionship, to the glorious western landscapes, to all the rises struck and missed.

It's amazing how much you remember. Every fish has a certain personality. If you hook a good fish, whether you land him or not, many years from now you will be able to ransack your memory and come up with all sorts of details about what happened right then, and what the rest of the day was like. You can replay those fish in your mind. The only parts you tend to forget are the unpleasant ones, like the times you caught none, or the times you got soaked in a storm. Fishing is kind of like having children—you soon forget, so you do it again.

Paul Schullery and I have collaborated before on a book, *Bud Lilly's Guide to Western Fly Fishing*, in which I relate what I think are the important things to know about how to catch trout here in the West. This book isn't more instruction, at least not like the *Guide* is. The *Guide* was written to tell you how I do it. This book is written to explain why it's meant so much to me.

Bud Lilly
Bozeman, Montana
Summer 1987

1

MONTANA BEGINNINGS

Bud Lilly, age one, Manhattan, Montana.

Mary Wells "Granny" Yates, late in her long and
adventurous life.

Bud Lilly and friends, about 1930.

Violet and Walen "Bud" Lilly, Sr.,
about 1935.

1942 was a good year for collecting memories of trout, deer, and elk, to help
carry me through the war.

9

Guiding sort of runs in my family. It began with our most famous and adventurous character, now remembered in this part of Montana as Granny Yates. Granny was born Mary Wells in Virginia in 1815. She was seventeen when she married her sister's widower, George Yates, after the family conducted a thorough search of the Bible to make sure it was okay for a woman to marry her former brother-in-law. After the wedding, they saddled up and rode the 1,600 miles to Jackson County, Missouri, where they settled, eventually adding nine more children to the widower's three. George died in the 1850s, and in 1863, when she heard about the gold strike in what would later become Montana, Mary took three of the boys (most of the children were grown by then) and joined a wagon train. They took six cows with them and used the rocking motion of the wagon to help churn butter, which they in turn sold to the other pilgrims.

She made so much money selling the cows in Virginia City, Montana that she could afford a trip back to Missouri in 1864. She picked up some more of the children on this trip and also began to accumulate knowledge of the trail, so that eventually she organized and guided wagon trains of emigrants. The best estimate from the family is that she made the crossing between Montana and Missouri thirteen times (she ended up in Montana, which would account for the uneven number), the last time by rail.

Granny Yates bridged the years from the beginning of the western pioneering period to the first years of this century, and she saw enormous changes in that period. On some of her western trips the parties were threatened by Indians; one of her sons was wounded in an attack on the Yellowstone River in 1866, and she hid her youngest in a flour barrel for fear he would be discovered and taken by the Indians if they succeeded in capturing the wagon train.

She also displayed the sort of enterprise needed to succeed in the old territories. She once brought three barrels of apples to Virginia City from Missouri and sold them to the miners in that rough new town for a dollar apiece. She knew that everything she brought along had to pay its way, and it was said that the lineage of many horses in the Gallatin Valley could be traced to the animals she brought across, riding them side-saddle. When she died in 1907, she was the matriarch of a large family, with more than sixty grandchildren and ninety great grandchildren scattered throughout the country between Missouri and the West Coast. One of those grandchildren was my mother, born Violet Collins in 1903.

My mother's side of the family was dominated by big, strong women. They seemed to be in the tradition of Granny Yates, who was such a legend in the family that when I was young I sometimes wondered if she hadn't pulled the wagon herself. I grew up surrounded by these women, who ruled over most family get-togethers. It made me a fairly quiet kid because whenever we went somewhere, I just sat there with wide eyes while the women boomed at each other.

My mother's family were not sportsmen at all. They were ranchers, and even today there seem to be a lot of ranchers who never hunt the wildlife that abounds on their land. They were hardy, ambitious people, but I got my interest in outdoor sports from my dad's side of the family.

My father's mother had two brothers who were professional outdoorsmen. A. R. (Amos) and W. A. Hague emigrated from family farms in Nebraska to the Yellowstone area, apparently in the 1880s. Amos established himself in the Yellowstone Valley north of Yellowstone Park, and his brother settled in St. Anthony, Idaho. According to records in the Yellowstone Park archives, both of them occasionally guided parties of tourists and sportsmen in the Park, but so far Amos is the one about whom we have the most information. He was a tall, strong man, ramrod straight and of firm principles. There are letters in the Park archives revealing that he and his brother both took considerable risk in reporting poaching activities they discovered near the Park. Amos was known to have taken many parties through Yellowstone Park back in the 1890s and afterwards, including some important parties of dignitaries.

He was still alive in the 1930s, which was when I met him.

My dad took me over to visit him in his cabin up in the hills west of Emigrant, Montana, in the Yellowstone River valley. He was a trapper and a professional hunter, and his cabin was a kid's idea of heaven, with furs and trophies all over the walls. I suspect that even then he was living off the land. He had a good many fine items that since have disappeared, including rifles and other gifts that were given to him by some of his more distinguished clients who, according to family tradition, included European royalty. I always thought I somehow inherited some of his characteristics in that I enjoy showing people the outdoors.

My dad was the son of a Nebraska corn farmer. He left a rough home life when he was twelve and apprenticed himself to a barber in Kearney, Nebraska, where his apprenticeship consisted of practicing on local jail prisoners. By the time he was sixteen he had his own barbering business.

He barbered around Nebraska until 1916, when he heard about a big dam project on the Owens River in California. This was the first big dam to be built in California, and he moved to Bishop that year. He was thirty-two at the time, and he made friends with an attorney in California who introduced him to fly fishing. He used to tell me stories of the fabulous fishing in California back in those days, when you could have some of the best trout streams to yourself. Those stories were part of the reason I was always so interested in fishing.

Dad had always been an avid outdoorsman even as a child. He had been a market hunter as a young man in Nebraska, shooting prairie chickens, ducks, and any other game that could be sold. He told me stories of going out with a spring wagon, his brother on one side of the wagon and him on the other, to hunt prairie chickens. One of his sisters would drive the wagon, and he and his brother would hunt the fields. By the end of the day, the wagon would be full of birds. He was a deadly shot, which was one reason I never got too excited about the shotgun. When we would go out hunting together, a bird would be dead as soon as it jumped up — before I could even swing my shotgun to it. He had no more mercy on me than he had on the birds; it was up to me to get a shot off first, and I hardly ever did.

As far as I knew, he was happy in California. He married there and had a daughter, but the marriage ended in divorce. Then, during World War I, he was a victim of the big flu epidemic that swept California, and the doctors suggested that he move to some place where he could convalesce and just do simple physical work. He had a relative near Bozeman, so he moved there and worked on a ranch for a year or two, doing as much fishing as he could in his free time.

He met my mother in about 1923 in Manhattan, where he had just opened a barbershop. He was in his early forties, and she was about twenty. His name was Walen, but everybody called him Bud. I was to be Walen, Jr., and of course would be called Buddy. They were calling me Buddy even before I arrived.

So in 1925 they had me, and my dad announced that I was enough and he didn't want any more. That's how he was able to devote a lot of his free time to taking me fishing and hunting, really instilling in me a love of the outdoors. I was an avid Boy Scout, and I loved anything to do with being outside.

I started to fish when I was still a small boy, probably not even school-age yet. Dad started me out in bait fishing, of course, and gradually got me involved in fly fishing. When I was about eight and could be trusted to ride a bicycle away from the house, I would ride down to the Gallatin River, which was only a mile from our house in Manhattan. On the weekend I'd often be there all day.

As long as I can remember, I was always engaged most by the instant of the strike. It doesn't matter how many thousands of trout I've taken since, I still have that same excitement whenever I put a fly over a trout and the miracle happens. I still react, in my mind and sometimes out loud, with something like, "Jesus! He took it! *He took it!*" There was a small creek called V Creek just on the edge of Manhattan, and just above the road bridge was a pool full of brook trout. The water was perfectly clear, and I could see those fish swimming around. I don't suppose any eight-year-old boy ever wanted anything more than I wanted to catch those fish. I would lie on the old plank bridge and feed a line down through a crack, staying as long as six hours to take a single fish. And when one would finally take it, I would be just amazed and thrilled. For me, at least, it's never changed.

Dad started me fly fishing as early as I could handle it. Having read all the outdoor magazines, I was familiar with fly fishing, but my exposure to it was limited to the old snelled wet flies until I got to West Yellowstone and opened my shop.

He wasn't influenced by eastern fishing at all. We got our tackle from South Bend and Horrocks-Ibbotson, and we had Perrine reels, and Martin and Meisselbach reels. For some reason Dad had decided that he liked automatics. My first was a Meisselbach, then I graduated to a South Bend Oreno-matic, then to a Perrine. My first fly rod was a telescopic Bristol steel rod. I don't know how much it weighed, but after a long, hot day of casting, it seemed to weigh about eight pounds.

On my thirteenth birthday my dad let me order a South Bend, nine-foot, three-piece split bamboo rod from Salt Lake City. It cost around twelve dollars. I've lost that rod, but I do have my first creel. You could put alligators in it. All I really needed for the summer was that rod, one of my reels, that laundry basket of a creel, and a few wet flies and snelled hooks. Heaven couldn't have offered a boy more.

Dad loved fly fishing, and was very good at it, but we were as open-minded as anyone at that time about tackle. We used bait or flies, depending upon the situation. If the water was fairly clear, we preferred flies, but if we had to use sucker meat, bullheads, worms, or grasshoppers, we didn't mind at all. We just loved catching fish.

Montana was not a place where you had to worry very much about what fly you were using, and I suppose that's why we developed such an independent set of flies. I doubt that I even knew that flies imitated certain aquatic insects; we used flies under some circumstances because they worked so well. The staple of our fly patterns was the series of flies developed by F. B. Pott. Pott had been a professional wigmaker, and he developed various techniques for weaving animal hair into fly bodies and hackles. I'm not sure he was the first, but of all the fly weavers in Montana, he was the most famous and successful, and we swore by his flies. I started with the woven-hackle Royal Coachman and the Mites—the Mr. Mite, Lady Mite, and Sandy Mite. Every now and then a new pattern would appear; I remember when the Graybacks were introduced. I thought it was a revolutionary event.

These were all just general attractor-type patterns. Pott apparently got the name of "mite" from "helgrammite," which was a local name for the nymphs of the large stoneflies (the helgrammite is actually the immature stage of the Dobsonfly, but that didn't matter to us). I don't know if Pott even knew that his flies often were pretty good imitations of stream insects; he just offered them all in about the same sizes and shape, so maybe it was just coincidence that some of the Mites were (and still are) excellent imitations of caddisfly larvae in their cases. He did offer a "rockworm" pattern that was pretty obviously an imitation of a cased caddis.

The Pott flies were expensive, usually about thirty-five cents each, at a time when most flies were ten cents apiece at most. I used to snag a lot of them in trees or in snags on the bottom, and my mother would ask me, "Can't you find something cheaper to lose?"

I'm sure that I was unaware of dry flies until well after World War II. I probably didn't learn about them until I bought my shop in West Yellowstone. The only fly we used that floated was the Bunyan Bug, a large, cork-bodied fly with horsehair wings that was developed by Norman Means of Missoula. Means was a famous Montana fisherman whose nickname was Paul Bunyan. He'd travel the state giving talks about fly fishing and promoting his series of bugs, and they were just what we needed. They came in several sizes and were an adequate imitation of the big stoneflies known as salmonflies. Most of the time during the salmonfly hatch we just used the naturals—we'd catch a couple of the big flies and put them on the hook. But the Bunyan Bugs were a great alternative.

Our technique was pretty simple. We always fly fished with a double- or a triple-fly cast of snelled wet flies, and fishing was a matter of throw it out there, let it sink, and hang on. When I started, the limit was twenty-five trout, and whitefish didn't count. I could catch all the whitefish I could carry back when I was ten years old, and I often marvel at the amazing fishing we had practically in our backyard.

It was a common practice to poach. When I was small I often fished with an old woman who was a friend of my mother. Ma Wiedman just loved to fish. The two of us would dig a can of worms in her chicken coop and go up to the Gallatin, this ten-year-old and his older friend, and we'd catch our twenty-five each in the morning, clean them, and go home for lunch. Then we'd go back and get another fifty in the afternoon. It was my job to try to pawn them off on the neighbors. It go so that often when I'd knock, they wouldn't answer the door. We flooded the locals with fish.

We had a lot of great fishing, but I don't know if it was really that much better then than now. There were so few laws regarding harvesting fish, and so little protection for streambeds and habitat, that many rivers are probably in better shape now than they were when Ma Wiedman and I were at our peak. But one advantage it certainly had was lack of company. My dad used to take me up the Gallatin Canyon for some fishing, and we were so spoiled that if we saw another fisherman, we considered it crowded. He complained that he didn't want to fish the Gallatin on the Fourth of July because he didn't want to break off the tip of his rod in somebody's ass. We had no idea how spoiled we were. I can imagine what he'd say if he were around today and could see the Henry's Fork during the Green Drake hatch, or the floaters on the Madison.

Baker Creek flowed right near Manhattan, and of course nobody back then had any idea that it would someday be a famous spring creek; it was just another creek like all the others around the valley. When I was about eleven, my Dad and I went down to fish the creek one summer evening. It was still a good creek, not yet being dewatered for irrigation, and we knew it had good fish in it. Just about dusk, he hooked a fish on one of the Potts flies, and the fish was too strong for him to land. By the time it was dark, he was still fighting it, so he sent me running back to the car to get the flashlight. I brought the light back and aimed it at the fish so we could at least get a look at it, but he finally landed it, well after dark. It weighed about nine pounds, the first really large brown trout I remember. Fish that big weren't routine, but they didn't cause much excitement around town, either. Fishing was just something people did; it wasn't news.

My own first experience with a large trout came about that same time, in Central Park, a little community between Manhattan and Belgrade. My grandfather had a butcher shop there, and in the summer I made the trip over now and then for the local fishing. There was a little spring creek that paralleled the highway through Central Park before flowing into the Gallatin River near town. It was just the right sized creek for a ten-year-old. It was lovely, full of watercress and perfectly clear, so clear that you could look in and see a batch of trout swimming around. If you pitched a grasshopper in, it would be a contest among the fish to get to it first; all you had to do was watch and set the hook. You'd yank back on the rod and they'd fly over you onto the highway, causing a good deal of confusion among passing motorists. I was fishing it one September day, just after school had started, and I didn't know that in the early fall big brown trout would come up out of the Gallatin into the creek to get ready for spawning. I was used to hooking little brook trout, maybe ten inches long, but when I tossed a grasshopper out there, a huge brown grabbed it. The weeds were really thick in the creek by then, so I knew that if he burrowed into the watercress he'd be gone. We didn't use delicate equipment in Montana in those days — the standard snelled hook had a leader of ten- or twelve-pound test — so I just hauled back and tossed this four-pound brown trout out onto the highway.

18

It was some years after that before I really understood about spawning runs. I remember the day vividly. It was October of my sophomore year in high school. I had played football the previous fall, but my dad decided that I was going to be such a great baseball player that he didn't want me getting hurt playing football. It was okay with me because it gave me a chance to do more fishing. One day my dad came home and said, "I was talking to Hayes, and he said that some of those holes in the river by his house are just full of trout. Why don't you go down and try it?"

I went down to the river right after school, put on a couple of wet flies, and pulled some line off my Oreno-matic reel. As soon as the flies hit the water, it looked like I'd thrown a dead chicken to a bunch of alligators. I hauled back and found myself attached to two big browns, weighing three or four pounds each. This was a new experience for Buddy. The trout were rolling around, pulling two ways at once, but as usual my leader was stout. So I got them up on the bank pretty quickly, threw my rod down, and jumped on them to wrestle them away from the river. I got them both, but when I tried to fish again I discovered I'd thrown the rod down too hard—the reel was bent and wouldn't work. I was so excited that I kept fishing anyway. I just pulled a whole lot of extra line out and kept it handy in case I needed it. I don't remember how many I kept except that I kept them all, big browns weighing up to four pounds. After that I was always aware of the spawning seasons of trout.

*   *   *

I had a second love as a teenager. I loved sports, especially baseball. Again, I owed my fondness for this pastime to my dad, who was an avid baseball fan. He was determined that I would become a major league ball player, which of course sounded like a great life to me, so whenever I wasn't fishing or in school, I played baseball. My dad let me just fish and play ball until the summer I was going on fifteen. Then I had to work and could play ball or fish only on Sundays and in the evening. I played on as many as three teams at once.

Manhattan had an independent baseball team that my dad more or less supported. He found a former pro pitcher who had a drinking problem and paid him twenty-five dollars a Sunday to pitch for us. The fellow was reliable enough that we won a lot and developed a reputation as one of the best teams in the state. Our biggest problem was finding a catcher who could hold this great pitcher, but once we did that we were hard to beat.

We didn't charge admission. We'd pass the hat, and though nobody had much money, we'd usually collect enough to pay the pitcher and a few other guys who demanded a little money. There was nothing in it for my dad except the joy of watching the game and placing an occasional bet. He'd bet on anything, even on whether or not little Buddy would strike out.

In the 1930s many of the great teams from the old black leagues did a lot of barnstorming, going through little towns all over the country picking up as many games as they could for a little money. I got to play against some of those great teams, and I always admired their spirit. Times had to be tougher for them than for the rest of us, and yet they'd show up at the big field where we played our games, park their cars under the trees, and have a picnic—they sometimes even had their families along—and just have a big time. I remember how I liked to listen to their talk, the women giving their men a hard time if they made an error, the kids running around and playing. It was our only exposure to a really different culture back then in Manhattan.

These were desperate times for the country, and some of the best ball players America ever produced were out on the road playing little local teams for a few bucks. These great black players had no chance to get into the majors back then, and so I suppose that the only good thing about it was that it did give a lot of guys like me the chance to play against really outstanding talents. I was playing on my dad's team of adults from the time I was thirteen, and besides our regular games against teams from Butte and Helena, we played the black teams whenever they came through.

I'm sure the high point of my baseball career was the day I batted against Satchel Paige. I don't even remember what team he was playing for, but I knew who Satch Paige was and had enough sense to be impressed. He would give me a big roundhouse curve and I'd almost fall on my face trying to get out of the way of it. I was only fifteen or so at the time, just a little over five feet tall, and his team thought it was hilarious that this team of Montana farmers had a little kid playing second base.

As good as he was, I did get on base. I suspect he let me hit because he thought I was cute, but however it happened, I ended up on first base with a ground ball single. I remember thinking that if I could get that far, maybe I could get farther, so after someone else advanced me to second, I decided to steal third. I guess I wasn't cute enough for that, because the third baseman was waiting with the ball when I arrived, and he just sort of scooped me up when I slid in.

We won enough games against other teams in the state and against the barnstorming teams that people started to hear about us in the cities. One Sunday two men showed up to see our team, and my dad didn't tell me that they were scouting us for the Cincinnati Reds. He introduced me to them after the game and told me that he would like me to take them fishing the next day. He was barbering and couldn't take the time off, so that was my first guiding experience. They were both fly fishermen from Salt Lake City, and they were really impressed with this teenaged kid who could catch so many fish. That seemed to impress them more than my ball playing.

About two years later they came back, and just as the war was starting, I signed a contract with the Cincinnati Reds system. They wanted me to be on line to play for the Salt Lake City farm team when I got out of high school, but of course the war changed a lot of our lives. By the time I got back, I'd lost interest in baseball. I had always played on teams of people mostly older than I was, and I never got over being a little gun-shy against the big pitchers. I held my own and was a very good fielder, but I knew my limitations.

The winter before my seventeenth birthday, the Navy was recruiting in our area. A friend came up to me at school one day and said, "Hey, let's go take this test — we can get out of school for two or three hours." I didn't even know what kind of test it was, but I took it. Soon after, I got notice that I'd passed the test and was invited to join a special Navy training program, which turned out to be the greatest thing that ever happened to me because it gave me the chance to get a college education. I signed up, and as soon as school was out I went to work for the Forest Service in the Cabinet National Forest out of Thompson Falls. I had worked there about three weeks, and was loving it, when my boss told me my letter had arrived — I was in the Navy.

I spent sixteen months at the old Montana School of Mines at Butte, getting an intensive introduction to engineering. Then I went to a midshipman's school at Throg's Neck, New York, an old Coast Guard school. I got my commission when I was nineteen and was sent to Florida for additional training in boats. There's more to education than class work, of course, and along the way I was learning about girls, and rental cars, and all sorts of things they hadn't been too talkative about back in Manhattan. I served for eighteen months in the South Pacific and was discharged from the Navy on June 12, 1946.

No sooner had I gotten home than my dad announced that we were going to fish the salmonfly hatch that weekend, and that was just the sort of announcement I wanted to hear. We fished right near Three Forks, using the naturals because the river was too muddy for fishing Bunyan Bugs on the surface. We used a two-fly cast — two Wright McGill snelled hooks with a couple of salmonflies on each hook. We'd put a big sinker on that rig, cast it out, and let it swing. I hooked one fish so large that he just took the line and went straight across the river and stayed there. I couldn't move him, even with the very heavy lines we used then, which I'm sure were at least ten- or twelve-pound test. To be back with the trout streams and trout that big was the greatest homecoming I could have imagined, and I spent about a month fishing until my dad, who didn't waste words, said, "Well, you've taken enough time off, now go to work."

About the middle of July I went to a barn dance down by Central Park. I had learned to drink fairly well in the Navy, so my friends and I were having a fine time when I saw this cute Irish girl dancing with some guy. I thought, "God, that's really neat." So I horned in and got a couple of dances. I found out that her name was Pat and that she worked for a doctor in Three Forks. The next day a friend and I drove down to Three Forks, hoping to find her. We pulled up and parked in front of the doctor's office. She later told me that when she saw us pull up, she decided that right then would be a good time to go across the street to the drugstore and get some cigarettes. When she came out in her cute little white uniform, we both effected a mutual show of surprise (sort of, "Well, hey, how are you?"), as if we both hadn't been trying to meet. We were married the following March.

In the late 1940s, when I was going to school at Bozeman, I very much wanted Pat to learn to fish. During the next couple of summers, we spent a lot of time fishing the Gallatin. There hadn't been much pressure on the river since before the war, so the fishing was outstanding everywhere.

But the income wasn't. I was on my way to becoming a teacher, but I knew that my salary wouldn't be good. I also knew that there was something else for me that I hadn't found yet. I also knew that it had to do with the outdoors.

Looking back now, it seems easy enough to see that I was headed in a certain direction. Recently my mother, who now lives in Three Forks (where she has been very active in preserving local history), gathered up a lot of things she'd saved from my childhood and showed them to Paul Schullery and me. Among them were all the usual trinkets and souvenirs, lots of photographs, Navy mementos, and so on, and a little three-ring notebook that was my first fishing log. It started in April of 1942, not long before I went into the Navy, and it had the kind of title page that only a child's bright ambition could produce. Written in pencil on the first page, between tiny black-and-white photographs of me and my dad outdoors, was this:

> This is a record of my excursions in the mountains and into field & stream.
>
> I like the good clean outdoors, wild game and all wildlife.
>
> My ambition is to always live in contact with wildlife.
>
> My hunting and fishing pardners, who are careful and considerate, are Don, Doug + *Dad*.
>
> This is from April 1, 1942 until Death.

Well, actually, it was only from April 1, 1942 until sometime in 1943, but the spirit was what counted, and it still holds true for me. In fact, it was one of the things that got me through the war. While in the Navy, I did what I suppose a lot of men did, I diverted myself by making a plan for the rest of my life. I decided that if I survived, I was going to go to Alaska. I wanted to do something in the outdoors in Alaska, though I wasn't sure what. All the time I was in the Navy, I read everything I could find about Alaska. Marriage and school sidetracked that ambition, but my ambition "to always live in contact with wildlife" never faded.

I got my degree in applied sciences in 1948, and I thought I was a pretty smart man by the time I started my teaching career in Roundup, Montana, a small ranching and mining community. I was twenty-two, and my first duty was to register my teaching certificate at the courthouse. I arrived in Roundup, found the county superintendent's office, and announced, "I'd like to register for school." The superintendent looked at this fresh-faced kid and asked, "Well, what grade are you in?" It took a minute to convince him I was a teacher, and even at twenty-two I was teaching some "kids" who were older than I was. It seemed there were quite a few who just liked staying in school, which I suppose was a lot nicer than going into the mines like their fathers.

I taught biology, chemistry, general science, and physics, and I was assistant basketball coach. I had the feeling that

I got all the courses that nobody else wanted, and I quickly realized that the teaching salary didn't stretch far enough. I also taught in Deer Lodge before settling in Bozeman in 1961, and by then I knew that I had to make more money.

A teacher friend of mine, Norm Hansen, told me about West Yellowstone one day. I don't know why it had occurred to him to tell me, or what had made him notice, but one day he pointed out to me that "Nobody in West Yellowstone will wash your car. They're all so busy pumping gas that you can't get a car wash. My mother has a little property there by the post office. Let's put up a little car wash."

So we went to West Yellowstone, cut a few trees for a tent, ran a garden hose from nearby, dug a drain ditch, and were in business. We'd wash cars from dawn until dark, and we eventually even put up lights so we could do it at night. One day I washed about eighteen cars and brought in more money than I was making as a teacher.

During that summer another friend said, "You know, there's a guy here that's a teacher in Billings who's going to be promoted to principal at the high school, and he'd like to sell his tackle shop. It's the one that Don Martinez started."

So I went over and looked at it, and I asked a friend to look at it. He said, "Well, you can buy it, but all you'll ever make is wages. It's just a little business." At that point, with my hands wrinkling up like prunes from all the car washing, wages sounded like a pretty good deal.

The shop was owned by Charles Borberg, who had tried to take over the Martinez reputation. Don still lived in California and still tied the flies for the shop, but he wasn't visiting much anymore. It looked like an interesting little business, but I had to agree that it didn't show much financial promise. I think I bought it for other reasons than the hope that it might make me a lot of money. I think I bought it because I could see West Yellowstone becoming a replacement for the Alaska dream; it would let me do what I wanted in the outdoors without even leaving my home state.

What I actually bought was the inventory, the sign, and a

walk-in cooler. I paid $4,500 for the whole show. I had about $2,000 that I'd saved for a car, but right then it was hard to find a car, so I had that money just sitting. My mother loaned me the other $2,500. My dad had died in 1948, and my mother had some insurance money that he had said she could give to me if I looked like I was going to do something productive with it. He believed in results.

I talked it over with Pat, and she encouraged me by saying that "If you want to buy it, I'll help you." I don't imagine she had any idea that she was offering to work like she did for thirty years.

I wrote the man a check for $4,500, and he said, "Do you want a receipt?"

"Well, I probably should have something." High finance in West Yellowstone.

"I'll give you a bill of sale," which sounded pretty impressive to me. He took a little piece of paper and wrote out a bill of sale on it. I was in business.

2

FIVE DOLLARS AND A CLEAN SHIRT

I was probably a little too skilled a fisherman
for the trout's good.

The original Trout Shop in the "off-season."

The Lunker Club was a center of attention in the shop; we posted many photographs of the best trout taken.

Poppy, official greeter at the Trout Shop, patrolled the floor while Pat was busy behind the "computer."

Charlie Brooks on a "Show-me" trip, seining
trout stream insects for his group to study.
Photos by Dr. James McCue.

Lefty Kreh, one of the greatest of all casting instructors,
demonstrating his low backcast for a group of students.
Lefty can cast so far that the fish are spoiled by the time
he gets them in. Photo courtesy of Fenwick/Sevenstrand.

Night-time visitors left their tracks in the snow in front of the Trout Shop. West Yellowstone is surrounded by excellent grizzly bear habitat.

Working late at the new shop. Photo by Greg Lilly.

When the Trout Shop was operating at its peak during the great fly-fishing boom of the 1970s, we put in long days. I usually got to the shop at about 6:45 A.M. The first thing I did was make five gallons of coffee, and by the time I had done that, the line had started to form. We had the steadies, sort of the Trout Shop Coffee Klatch, who showed up when we unlocked the door for the early social hour, which seemed to last until about lunchtime.

The guides showed up at 7:00 A.M. Their clients had been told to meet them at the shop, and each guide's assignment for the day was posted, along with a suggested trip for that day. The clients and guides knew each others' names in advance. The guides had a checklist of what to make sure the clients had before leaving the shop, most of it routine, like making sure they had the right flies for that day's fishing. But within a few minutes after seven, we'd have eight guides and twice as many clients foraging here and there, picking out a few of this and a few of that, and the cash register would start to sing. The guides were trained as salesmen, and they knew our inventory and our prices; that isn't as mercenary as it might at first seem because the clients were generally pretty insistent that they be properly outfitted, and spending a little more after they'd already spent a lot to get there and to hire a guide didn't seem like a problem to them. We just made it as easy as we could.

We would have five or six people writing up the purchases and twice that many calling from various parts of the shop to put them down for six of this and ten of that. I had this old gas station adding machine on the counter that required pulling the handle every time you added a number. First thing in the morning, when all these people were milling around getting ready to go out, and the first early customers were drifting in, and the store staff was bustling around tripping over each other and a dog or two, someone would come up to me and ask how I kept track of 3,000 items in the store and all these people buying and renting. I'd tell them I had a computer. This was when computers were still pretty exotic, and they'd light up and say, "Really? Where is it?", assuming we had some kind of big electronic thing in the basement. I'd give another yank on the handle of the adding machine and say, "Right here."

We'd have the clients and their guides. We'd have three or four people downstairs starting their day at the fly-fishing school. Mike might be getting someone ready to go backpacking into the Beartooth. Annette and Bonnie would be getting their ladies-only clients ready to go. Steve and Bonnie Billeb would be going over last-minute preparations for their head-waters camping trip group. I would stand in the middle of all that chaos and enjoy the cash flow, hoping we were getting receipts for most of it, at least.

The only disadvantage was that until all the guides cleared out about nine o'clock and the feeding frenzy kind of quieted down, the drop-in customer was likely to get neglected. There was just too much going on for us to handle any more.

The biggest challenge was keeping track of that much money being collected in a short time. Twenty or so fly fishermen fresh from the city and anxious to make the most of their fishing can be world-class impulse shoppers. If we had a full load of clients, we might have cleared $5,000 by nine o'clock in the morning. At that point, anything we took in during the rest of the day seemed like bonus money.

We worked both sides of the street; we had a good selection of spinning tackle as well as the fly-fishing tackle, and we always had at least one clerk like Chuck Johnson who was a whiz with spinning gear and could help the spin fishermen. We always had someone knowledgeable about backpacking, too, because we carried so much outdoor clothing and back-packing gear.

We kept the coffee and cookies for customers all day, every day. We fed every Boy Scout in America. They would pull up in big buses just for the cookies at the Trout Shop. I still don't know how they sniffed us out, but they didn't buy much tackle.

It stayed busy all day. There was no such thing as a reasonable break, and the business didn't arrange itself conveniently so that anybody could sit down and eat a civilized lunch. It seems to me now that during the years the shop was doing well, I ate about 9,000 hot dogs. Finding time for lunch was a problem.

Business did begin to taper off by four o'clock, and then about five we'd get an hour or so of rush from the guys who were going out for the evening fishing. After that, staying open was mostly a matter of doing the locals a favor by providing them with a place to come in and try on hats.

Late in the day, sometime after dark, the late shift of the coffee klatch would show up to talk over the day. It had been tradition in West Yellowstone to stay open until ten o'clock, but we gradually realized that we could close at nine, then at seven, with no harm to our business. But there were many evenings even then when I'd promise Pat we'd get out early, and at seven o'clock I'd still be standing there dispensing tackle and information like I'd just arrived.

I hated to close the shop in the evening. I'd just be about to turn off the sign and lock up when here would come some bleary-eyed guy who'd just driven three thousand miles and wanted to get an early start tomorrow and could he just pick up a few things and oh, by the way, how's the fishing been?

The guides would start dragging in between seven and eight to report on their day's fishing. I would have spent the day gathering random information from fishermen, so between what I had picked up and what the guides brought in, we had an unusually good idea of what the next day's fishing possibilities would be. That network of information gathering gave us a real edge over the other shops. The last few years, Greg was in charge of the guides, so he would check them all in and learn all that he could from them about fishing conditions. Then about ten o'clock that night, he and I would sit down at the kitchen table and go over all we'd learned that day about fishing in the area. Then we would plan the next day's trips, matching each client's personality, interests, and skills with the right guide and the right fishing. About ten-thirty or eleven we would call it a day. As I collapsed into bed, I would sometimes wonder if success was such a great thing after all. It had all been a lot simpler back in the beginning.

*　　*　　*

The early 1950s were still a time of pioneering in fly fishing around our part of the country. People had been fly fishing in the West for a long time, but as far as a commercial enterprise, it was only beginning to show its potential. Dan Bailey had opened his shop in Livingston some years earlier, and Bob Carmichael and Boots Allen and a few others were making a go of it in Jackson. West Yellowstone had a few shops and guides, but they catered to a much smaller and more exclusive crowd.

West Yellowstone, right at the west entrance to Yellowstone National Park, had not shown much sign that it would eventually become the western Mecca of fly fishing. The first real fly shop of which I know was Vint Johnson's, which was opened in about 1941. Vint started his shop in a corner of Fuller's Garage. The story goes that he opened up, went up to Billings and bought a pile of merchandise, came back, and sold it all on the Fourth of July. He had to go back to Billings for more.

His place was called the Tackle Shop, and though Vint was himself a fly fisherman, he knew enough to cater to all the interests he could. So he sold bait and lures, as well. Vint was one of the first West Yellowstone fishermen to get any national exposure. He had the good fortune to get written up by the great Ray Bergman (longtime fishing editor for *Outdoor Life*), who fished with Vint and who over the years wrote some wonderful things about fishing in the Yellowstone area.

But the first West Yellowstone fisherman to really establish himself as an important fly tier and authority was Don Martinez. Don was the original owner of the Trout Shop, the store I acquired in 1950, and for many years he ruled the fly-fishing scene there, especially as that business concerned wealthy and influential visiting fishermen. Like Carmichael down in Jackson, who was his friend, Don had become established as the man to see concerning fishing. He was only interested in fly

36

fishermen, and he was one of the top fly tiers and fly-tying theorists of his time. It's a shame his skills aren't better remembered now because his flies were excellent, and his knowledge of the insect life of the Yellowstone area was extraordinary. He took entomology seriously and developed many excellent flies, including a series of mayfly nymphs, his Multi-colored Variant dry flies, some fine cranefly nymphs, and of course one of America's most famous flies, the Woolly Worm, which he refined from an earlier pattern and introduced in its present form. The Woolly Worm alone should entitle him to a front-row seat among angling history's luminaries, and it probably would if he'd had the good taste to develop it in New York or Pennsylvania where more people would have sung its praises in print.

As I said, Don was only interested in fly fishermen, and he had little use for other kinds of fishing. The crowd of regulars who fished the West Yellowstone area then was pretty highbrow by modern standards, sort of typified by the attitudes and writing in Howard Back's lovely little book, *The Waters of Yellowstone with Rod and Fly* (1938). They were few in number, they prided themselves on their fine tackle, and their circle was pretty much closed to newcomers or people who fished differently than they did. One of Martinez's most famous remarks was that the bait-fishermen came to town with five dollars and a clean shirt, and they didn't change either one. It wasn't a situation where it was easy to break in with a new tackle shop. The fly fishermen knew where they would spend their money, and the bait fishermen didn't spend enough to make any difference.

The first man to make a significant dent in the Martinez hold was Pat Barnes, who by the time I arrived had to a great extent replaced Don as the reigning expert in town. He had a lock on the fly-fishing business, at least among the affluent clients. Pat's father and uncle both had many connections in Chicago, and they had done a lot to help connect Pat with sportsmen from the Midwest and East. Pat taught school in West Yellowstone a year or two and worked in the summers for

Don Martinez before going on his own. By the late 1940s he was way ahead of any other guide in the area.

Among other things, Pat should probably get the credit for first bringing the McKenzie boats to our part of Montana and thus popularizing that kind of float trip. The McKenzies didn't take over instantly, and they still share the river with rafts and johnboats. Merton Parks, who came out to Gardiner, Montana from Minnesota, was a real booster of the john-boats, and he gave me my first lesson in them. I asked him if he'd show me how he floated with them, and he said he would if I'd give him a tour of the Henry's Fork at the same time. One pretty day in early June we put in at Last Chance, Idaho and spent a lovely day floating along. The fishing was slow, but we were too busy marveling at how we had the river to ourselves to notice. When we floated up to the Osborne Bridge we saw a big sign that said: "Fishing Season Opens June 15." Suddenly we understood why we had the river to ourselves.

Anyway, when I first opened the door to my shop in 1950, I could see that the competition wasn't going to do me too many favors. There wasn't much business to go around, and it took many years to slowly break in to those exclusive circles and gain the trust and respect of the fishermen. In the mean-time, I spent a lot of time sitting on the fence outside my door gossiping with the man who owned the little curio shop next door. This man was so fatalistic about business that he really wasn't too interested in being bothered by customers. If, while we were sitting there, someone would come by and act like he or she were going to walk into his shop, he'd say, "Wait a minute; don't go in there! Tell me what you want; maybe I don't have it." He wasn't the most inspiring role model for a new merchant.

We were all looking for ways to attract attention. In Jackson Hole, the Humpy, a fly based on an earlier pattern called the Horner Special (developed by Jack Horner of San Francisco), became all the rage. In order to sell more of them, the shopowners introduced them with different-colored bodies,

which probably made no difference at all to the fish. It was
a great fly pattern, whatever color you made it, and they were
sold by the millions. Boots Allen used to put them out in nail
kegs—a keg full of green-bodied Humpies, a keg full of red-
bodied Humpies, and so on—and people would just grab a
handful, saying, "I'll take these." Western fishing was still fairly
short on theory, despite the best efforts of Martinez.

It's hard to imagine, now, just how little was known
about fishing in the area. I suspect that the competition between
the shops and guides had a lot to do with the rapid pace of
progress we've made since then. For instance, when I came to
town, many of the serious visiting fly fishermen still followed
the British approach of fishing only the rise. They would go
out to the rivers, and if they saw no fish rising, they would
come home. They might all be back in West Yellowstone by
noon. "Well, the hatch is over," they'd announce, and they'd
take a seat until that evening or the next day. Many of them
wouldn't use nymphs or streamers. Many of them probably
didn't know about them.

That changed dramatically in the 1950s, as more and more
dry-fly patterns, streamers, and other flies were developed or
brought in and as technological advances, especially the
popularization of spin fishing and the advent of the fiberglass
rod, made trout fishing more accessible to more people.
Coupled with that was our constant effort to attract attention
to our businesses, and I guess that's where I found I had an
edge. I seemed to have a knack for figuring out ways to make
customers happy and keep them coming back.

I could see that Martinez and Bob Carmichael, over in
Moose, Wyoming, were very successful with a personal
approach. Selling fly-fishing tackle wasn't like selling pharma-
ceutical products; people wanted to talk, and they wanted to
get to know you. I made an effort to talk to everybody who
came in, and because I was blessed with a good memory, I
accumulated a lot of information about just where the fishing
was good, and what flies or techniques were working, and
all of that. In that way the shop became a real clearinghouse

of information, which benefited us and the customers. It may have benefited my son Greg most of all because while I was standing in the shop talking all summer long, he was out guiding and fishing every day, putting all those ideas into practice. That's one reason he is a much better fisherman than I am today. He has an adjustability that few other fishermen can match; he can find a way to solve the problem.

Of course, the other good thing about having that kind of memory was that it was great for customer relations in general. There was a Baptist minister who came to West Yellowstone as part of a revival, and he loved to fly fish. He often came into the shop when he wasn't working, and though I'm sure he didn't know it, he was very easy to remember. He had a hat covered with flies and an accent you could cut with a crosscut saw, so he stood out like the proverbial turd in a punchbowl. Then, about ten years went by, and one day he strolled in the shop again. I looked up and said, "Could I help you, Reverend?" He almost fell over.

During the early 1950s, I began to keep a record of anyone who caught a trout weighing three pounds or more. We called it the Lunker Club and encouraged customers to sign it. We'd record the date, the species of fish, where it had been caught, and what had been used to catch it. Unlike Dan Bailey's very famous Wall of Fame up in Livingston, we didn't differentiate between methods. To qualify for Dan's Wall you had to take the fish on a fly, and if it was taken from a stream, it had to weigh at least four pounds. We accepted fish for the Lunker Club if they were caught on bait, lures, or flies, and if they were kept or released. The interesting thing was that the people who took time to register a big fish were usually fly fishermen. The bait fishermen and lure fishermen didn't bother, being interested mostly in meat in the first place.

The Lunker Club was such a useful promotion because we had a little pennant that was awarded to the most recent entry. The fisherman could put it on his car aerial, but most of them let their motel have it to display for their customers. That was the best we could hope for because it got the motels involved, which in turn meant that their guests would be hearing about the Trout Shop.

Of course, we were always looking for promotional ideas, and many of the best were provided free by various tackle manufacturers. Their representatives came to town regularly to put on demonstrations, which were always good for gathering a crowd even if it was only the local boys with nothing better to do. One summer a man named Warden came around giving demonstrations with a reel that was detached from the rod. You wore the reel on a harness that was strapped around your body. The reel was a free-spooling model that was mounted in the middle of your chest, with line running to the rod, which you held in your right hand. Warden got himself all trussed up in this rig and gave a demonstration in the street in front of my shop one day, and it was true that he could practically throw a casting plug out of sight. He was really impressing the crowd; quite a few tourists had gathered to watch this expert, who was all outfitted in his waders and everything. In fact, his show was a big success until someone called out, "That's a great outfit, but what do you have to do if you want to take a shit?" That really dampened the spirit of the group, and we didn't get any orders for Mr. Warden's outfit.

I guess our biggest and most effective promotional effort in those early years was our map. We reprinted Don Martinez's little fishing map for the Yellowstone area and distributed it by the thousands. In 1960 I revised it, and with the help of Dave Bascom (better known to fishermen as Milford Poltroon, editor of the *Wretched Mess News*), designed a new map more to our liking. Dave was a successful California advertising executive who loved fly fishing and who was an able copywriter. The entire map was littered with the most wonderfully silly remarks, like:

> For years now, writers in *Field & Stream*, *Outdoor Life*, and *Sports Afield* have been bragging so loud about the terrific fishing hereabouts, it's sort of inspired the fish, given them something to live up to. And around this neck of the woods, The Trout Shop is generally acknowledged as offishal fishing head-

quarters. In fact, FISH KNOW if you've been here first, and if
you haven't, they're likely to fin their noses at you.

So first thing to do when you arrive in West Yellowstone is
visit The Trout Shop. Get your license (no license required in
Park), get free current fishing regulations, swap lies, etc. NOTE:
I will listen to all your fish stories with a straight face. *No
other tackle shop can make this claim.* I promise not to pressure
you to buy a single doggone thing. You're welcome if all you
want is free directions, advice, or to escape from a charging
moose. (No moose can charge in The Trout Shop, and neither
can you. Cash only.)

Those maps traveled far, and by 1970 we were giving
away 10,000 of them a year. They were handy for use in the
shop because we could make notes on them for the visiting
fishermen, showing them which general areas were good.
They were great also for sending to people who asked questions
by mail. We didn't have a handier educational tool until the
catalog came along, but that's getting a little ahead of my story.

I had been teaching at Deer Lodge for nine years by
1959, and the tackle business was picking up, so I decided to
try to make a complete living from it. I quit my teaching job
that year, but as practically everyone from our part of the
country knows, Providence took a hand in the local economy
that year. The famous earthquake of 1959 killed many people
in a campground downstream from Hebgen Lake. The land-
slide created Quake Lake by damming the Madison River, and
the quake messed up the fishing in many parts of the region.
Even if people weren't too scared to come and fish, they might
not find much worth doing when they got here. Business in
West Yellowstone was bad for a few years before it gradually
recovered, but at the time of the quake I'd already sold my
house in Deer Lodge. So I was lucky to find work in Bozeman
at the university, working as a biological assistant for profes-
sors doing research. I grew very tired of Petri dishes.

In 1960 I tried a year in Scottsdale, Arizona, teaching high
school. That came about because of my son Mike's health
problems. His doctor suggested we try a drier climate, but it

turned out to be unnecessary for Mike and unbearable for the rest of us. So then I came back to Bozeman and taught for nine more years at Bozeman Junior High School, retiring in 1970 as it became clear we could develop the shop into a year-round business. Everyone who fished through the 1970s knows that it was the decade of great growth in fly fishing, and we were ready when it started. The young Lillys had grown up and were able to take a share of the business of the shop, and we older Lillys had twenty years of experience under our belts. It was an enormously exciting time, exhausting and fulfilling at once. Suddenly there were writers appearing who had spent the sixties patiently studying insects and trout and who were now ready to publish their results. New fly patterns, new rods, new reels, and new ideas appeared regularly. A lot of what happened was hype, but much of it was important, too, and it was a great time to be running the Trout Shop.

In 1967 we had moved from our cramped quarters in the little shop in what is known as the "Eagle's Corner" of West Yellowstone (the Eagle family have been storekeepers in town for many years) to the shop's present location in a much larger, more roomy building. This gave us the room to meet all the new needs of fly fishermen in the new era that dawned about the time Swisher and Richards' *Selective Trout* was published, in 1971.

So much was happening. The campaign for special regulations was gathering force, the Park was rewriting its regulations, the Federation of Fly Fishermen (now the Federation of Fly Fishers, FFF) and Trout Unlimited (TU) were gaining a national audience, and local fly-fishing clubs were springing up everywhere. Swisher and Richards, Dave Whitlock, I, and many others began to make speaking tours, talking about western fishing and inviting people to come try it. It all fit into my various schemes to promote fly fishing and do some business at the same time.

Our guiding, gradually increasing through the 1960s, really took off. We started our guide trips in May, and we would be busy until late October. More and more people were visiting our area in the off-season. In the fall we were especially busy. There was no break in our traffic after Labor Day, as many of the regular visitors knew that that was when the tourist traffic eased up and the fishing started to improve in the cooler weather.

We were lucky to have some really great guides working for us, but I always felt that Greg and Mike and Barry were probably the best. There were others who were as good at guiding, but my two sons and my son-in-law were really loyal and became the most popular with the clients. People practically fought over them — who was going to go with one, and who was going to go with another.

We reached the point in the 1970s where we practically commanded the guide business in West Yellowstone. Pat Barnes had his own very good, carefully chosen clientele, but we had such a demand that we'd book all our own guides, eight or ten of them, and then we'd call around and book everyone else's with our overflow.

But it seemed as if there were more opportunities for us and for fly fishers than just the guiding business, and it was here that I think the Trout Shop really set itself apart. We organized the second set of fly-fishing schools in this country after Orvis had started theirs in 1966. I could see that Orvis had a good idea, and that there had to be a market for something similar in the West. The first schools we set up were in cooperation with Phil Clock of Fenwick in 1969. We had Jimmy Green and Lefty Kreh, two of the greatest casting instructors in the world, running the classes, and it cost only about twenty-five dollars. It had to be one of the great bargains in fly fishing.

The schools were an incredible opportunity for people to learn a lot from the best fishermen. We had various representatives from the tackle companies (maybe Lefty Kreh and Ben Silkknitter from Scientific Anglers, and Hugh Reilly, Jimmy Green, or Phil Clock from Fenwick), and they not only were outstanding fishermen and instructors, they were great salesmen. If you watch Lefty cast for about five minutes, you'll be ready to buy anything he's got. I think a lot of people didn't realize how much expertise they were getting for their money, though looking back now we can see how rare that kind of gathering of talent is. The tackle companies participated for the promotional aspects of it, and we all benefited. We'd have a school of thirty or thirty-five people, and we'd do five or six thousand dollars' worth of business in tackle before the school was over.

Of course, eventually Fenwick set up its own schools on the edge of town, and gradually other competition developed, but we had a lot of fun anyway, getting all those great fishermen together.

After the schools were going, I began to cook up more specialized sessions. We offered what we called angling rendez-vous, where a few advanced fishermen would pay for an intensive fly-fishing session with some well-known angler. We had Doug Swisher and Carl Richards, Ed Koch, Ed Shenk, Charlie Brooks, and Ernie Schwiebert, which gave people an opportunity to spend a day or two with their favorite authors and get a firsthand experience with their expertise. That was a very popular program, though not especially successful financially because there were just too few customers involved to bring in enough money to pay everybody who needed to be paid. But I think of the opportunity it gave fishermen to attend a clinic with an acknowledged master, or several of them, and it seems like it was worth a try. The students certainly thought so.

Then we developed the clinic, with Berkley and other companies. It differed from the schools in that it was a one-day intensive program where several companies would send their representatives and they'd all introduce the people to a variety of techniques and tackle.

When Charlie Brooks's book, *Larger Trout for the Western Fly Fisherman*, came out, it occurred to me to have a sort of "show-me" trip, where the author would take a few people out and show them all the things that they'd read in his book. That didn't work out as well as some of the programs because the people didn't catch as many trout as they must have expected; Charlie was trying to concentrate on acquainting them with the stream ecology aspects of fishing and didn't get them into fish the way they wanted. We got a few complaints from people who felt they'd not gotten the fishing experience they wanted, so eventually we abandoned that program.

The show-me trips were a great bargain for the customers. The chance to spend a day with Charlie, or Dave Whitlock, or Ernie Schwiebert, for only the regular guide fee, was a rare gift in fly fishing, and a lot of people found it very rewarding.

My daughter Annette and Bonnie (Greg's wife) ran the ladies-only trips, where a woman was able to go out with a woman guide, no husband around looking over her shoulder or screaming at her. It provided the woman fly fisher with several things, including a lot of good instruction and the chance to see a woman who had mastered fly fishing and become an accomplished angler. A few other guides worked for us in this program, including Lynn Corcoran who, with her husband Dave and my son Greg, now operate the River's Edge shop in Bozeman. They'd start with a short session in the shop, demonstrating knots and talking a little about flies, depending upon the client's experience, and then go to the Firehole or the Madison or some other stream for some fishing.

Mike and Barry took people on backpacking trips, and I think we were among the first in the area to offer trips of that sort. We specialized in high-country lake fishing in the Beartooth region northeast of Yellowstone Park. It's some of the wildest, most beautiful country in the world, with hundreds of small lakes with cutthroat, golden, and brook trout fishing in a spectacular setting.

We also had some very successful trips to the headwaters of the Yellowstone. This involved a boat and canoe trip to the southeast arm of Yellowstone Lake in the Park, one of the most isolated parts of the Park. We'd precook a lot of things and then take steaks and other fresh food packed in dry ice, so that the whole five days was very comfortable. We'd have the guide bake biscuits in a reflector oven, so all the rustic touches were there.

We'd establish a base camp along the lake, then make short trips up into tributaries of the lake for some of the wildest fishing imaginable. These were all cutthroat trout, part of the greatest remaining pure cutthroat fishery in the country. The fishing was sometimes very easy, which it sometimes can be with wilderness fish. There was a cutthroat in Mountain Creek that they marked the first time they caught him, and in the course of a five-day camp, they caught him a total of twelve times. Fishing doesn't get much more pristine than that.

I sent a man and wife team to this camp, Steve and Bonnie Billeb, both of whom were trained naturalists. Steve was a botanist, Bonnie a zoologist, and both had taught on the university level. The people got a great all-around experience, not only the fishing but everything about the place was shown to them. There was a doctor from Bakersfield, California who enjoyed the trip so much that two years in a row he bought the whole trip for himself and his wife. He would pay the cost of guiding six or eight people just so he and his wife could enjoy all that service, attention, and grandeur.

We had a twenty-seven-foot trailer that we would use to take three or four people for four or five days and move around to different rivers. I'd send along a cook, and it was very popular. We'd do it only in the fall, when other things were kind of slow. Usually those trips were booked up a year in advance.

What we developed out of this program was a broader approach to western fly fishing than was being promoted by anyone else. We made "Western Fly Fishing—The Total Experience" a sort of informal motto for the shop, and we firmly believed in convincing people that this wasn't just a place to come and catch trout. We sold field guides, backpacking gear, and many nonfishing items, but this was never just a matter of finding new ways to make money. Our whole family loved the West for many reasons not having to do with fishing, and we wanted to share those things. It's amazing, for example, how many fishermen come to Yellowstone Park for twenty or thirty years to fish and after all that time they still know practically nothing about the Park and all its natural wonders. We wanted to change that, and to persuade people to take some time out to enjoy the surroundings of western fishing as much as they did the fishing. I think we had some success.

The new part of the business of which Pat and I were probably proudest was the art gallery. We opened the gallery in the early 1970s. By the time we sold the shop, it was pretty well established. That was a fun part of the business. It wasn't a great money-maker, but it paid its way, and we enjoyed broadening the business. Pottery was usually what sold best, and people bought hundreds of those rocks painted like animals. We concentrated on local artists, getting to know some wonderfully talented people, some of whom have gone on to earn national reputations. These were unusual directions for a western tackle shop, but they brought us a lot of joy, while substantially broadening the business. That's a hard combination to beat.

But our biggest business adventure was our catalog. Mail order was old news in 1969, but we saw some great opportunities for our little shop in catalog sales. So we embarked on what was a completely amateur program that turned into a more successful business than we ever would have dreamed. We were pretty conservative. I imagine that if we'd jumped into mail order, we could have grown faster than we did. If we'd gone to professional procedures and the buying of lists and all of that, we could possibly have done more. But what we did we seemed to do well.

The first catalog came out in about 1969. I had no experience in catalogs whatsoever. All I knew was that it was time to publish a catalog. So I started cutting pictures out of other people's catalogs, sticking them on a piece of paper and writing a little copy. Peter Alport's handbook from his Wyoming Outfitter's shop was more or less my model. It was a mix of products and useful information, and that was always the idea with the Trout Shop's catalog. Every year I'd write up some short items about the fishing and the new flies and such to mix in with the products. We cultivated a very hospitable and conversational tone in the catalog, and many people told us how they looked forward to it each year.

We started with a small list of about 3,000 names gleaned from fishing license sales and the Lunker Club book. Somewhere I had heard that I needed to get a bulk mailing permit, but I didn't know anything about sorting. We simply addressed 3,000 catalogs, threw them in sacks, and hauled them over to the post office. The post office people had fits, and we had to drag them all back and presort them by zip code, just like real mail-order outfits were expected to do.

The catalog became our official voice. It let us keep people up-to-date on the rivers, on developments in our family, and on all the new products that were flooding the market. I went out of my way to include lots of pictures that had no real product orientation: fishing scenes, insect photography, and so on. Just the other day I heard that early copies of the catalog (its full name was *Bud Lilly's Tackle Catalog and Handbook for Western Trout Fishing*) are appearing in used angling-book catalogs for five dollars. I should have kept more of them.

I suppose I knew we had really arrived when Arnold Gingrich praised the handbook in *The Joys of Trout* (1973):

> Bud Lilly's Trout Shop for the past twenty years has been a virtual gateway to paradise for fly fishermen . . . His tackle catalog and handbook for western trout fishing is the best I know. But send for it at your own risk, as it's highly infectious. Don't say I didn't warn you, that you'd better be prepared, before you open its covers, to be lured into a trip to Montana. Few better fates, however, could befall a fly fisher.

Of course, it didn't take too much of that kind of talk to make the catalogs even more popular. By the time I sold the shop in 1982, the mailing list was up to 30,000 names.

* * *

Being in a retail business is a great course in human nature. If you don't basically like people, you probably have no business standing behind a counter selling them stuff. Fly fishermen are interesting, and knowing them, meeting them in the shop all those years, was a great experience. Oh, sure, some people demand too much, like the guy who wants to get you over in the corner for an hour or so and get detailed instructions on how to tie a fly, or the person who wants to debate the qualities of different hackles for two or three hours. Once in a great while I had to get pretty rude to get someone to let us get on with our work and help other people.

Perhaps the most surprising tackle shop characters were the people who hardly ever seemed to fish. They'd come to town for a couple weeks and spend the first few days just getting ready. This is no exaggeration; they might spend a day or two just tying up leaders in the motel. They'd come in to all the shops, gathering information about the fishing. I suppose they wanted to know exactly what it was they weren't doing. They would go from tackle shop to tackle shop, asking the same questions so they could compare information. I'd go through my spiel, answering some fishing question, and they'd nod happily and say, "Yes, that's what they told me at the last place."

For others the tackle shop was a social gathering place. They seemed to get up in the morning, put their vest on, and then just wear it all day. They were attracted to fishing by the society of it, which is something most of us are interested in, but most of us kind of like to fish, too. This sort of person would get to the tackle shop and just hang around until a conversation started up in which they could get involved. One conversation might be good for two or three hours.

I didn't really mind this type, because I'd also get people who wanted to spend an hour or two going over their fishing that day on a minute-to-minute basis. When I could see I'd been captured by one of those, I'd say, "Wait a minute; I've got a friend over here who knows all about that," and I'd call the conversationalist over and introduce him to the detail man. It was sort of like introducing a sadist to a masochist; here were people who could really *satisfy* each other. Two hours later they'd still be deep in their discussion. It was almost a community service I performed, getting these people with common interests — one wanted to talk, one wanted to listen — together. They'd just about wear out our wall map with their fingertips, following various streams here and there.

But people like those were the exception. Most of the time there was really no telling the customers from the friends. We always got our greatest satisfaction as shopowners, and our greatest pleasure as fly fishers, from being able to put someone in the right place for some good fishing. There's nothing more rewarding than to have people come back voluntarily and go out of their way to thank you for putting them on to some good fishing. We loved it when someone would come in and say, "Thank God for you; you just saved our whole trip — we'd had four days of no luck at all and you sent us to a great spot."

Possibly the nicest testimonial I ever received came from Reverend Dan Abrams, a fine gentleman and fly fisherman from Jackson Hole. He moved to the West some years ago and came into my shop for some advice. A story like the one below (which was part of a column he wrote for one of the Jackson newspapers) goes a long way in convincing me that the early mornings and the late evenings were more than worth it.

> When the family and I finally got to make the long-planned trip, one of the first things I did was to drag them off to the Lilly's Trout Shop. After I told Bud I had driven over 2,000 miles for a taste of his famous waters, I thought he would send me immediately to the Madison, suggest the Firehole, or at least point me in the direction of the Yellowstone. He courteously answered all my questions about these well-known streams, but then, looking at my two young boys and travel-weary wife, he advised me to consider another possibility.
>
> "Look," he said, "my wife and I just returned from a two day stay at a tiny Forest Service campground containing but three sites along the Gallatin between here and Bozeman. It's a great place for the whole family to relax and enjoy. The scenery is impressive and the fishing is interesting."

"Interesting?" I asked. "What do you mean by that?"

Bud just smiled and said, "I think you'll find it to your liking. Here, I'll draw you a map showing you exactly how to find the spot."

We left the shop, grateful for the tip and amazed that anyone would share one of his favorite fishing holes with a friend he'd known for only fifteen minutes.

3

A FLYFISHING
FAMILY

The family in the late 1970s, from left: Annette, Greg, Pat, Bud, and Mike.
This picture was taken during a Conclave of the FFF, and we were all
exhausted from guiding, giving talks, and running the shop. Poppy
maintained her usual calm.

Greg, eight, and Mike, six.

Mike, six, showing his catch in the Trout Shop.

Annette grew to be a fine fly fisherperson and a popular guide.

The whole family doubled as models in our catalog.

Greg casting during a Bud Lilly/Berkley clinic.

Mike, left, and Greg, were both experienced and sought-
after guides by the time they were twenty.

It was always the family that made the Trout Shop matter. I don't mean that the shop mattered because it helped support the family, though that was also true; I mean that the Trout Shop, with its long hours and all the rest, became such a central part of our lives because we were all involved. We did it together, and I can't imagine a finer thing a family could say than that.

Greg was born in 1949, and Mike and Annette came along after the shop was in operation, Mike in 1952 and Annette in 1955. I don't know now how we found time to run both the shop and the family, but I do know that we were lucky things didn't get really busy in the shop until the kids were older. Those first few years were pretty slow going for the business.

But life could hardly be called routine in West Yellowstone, even for such a small town. For one thing, there were the bears. There were grizzly bears using the dump north of town every night until the early 1970s, and they were often seen in town at night (they still are), as were the smaller black bears. The black bears would get especially bold during the day, and sometimes we'd have to chase them away. I sold wrist rockets (very powerful slingshots) in the shop, and if you hit a black bear once or twice with a rock or a marble, it would usually go away. I remember one day the kids were out playing in the yard, and a black bear climbed a lodgepole pine right next to the yard. He just sat there watching them. There aren't many things that would make a parent more nervous, so I gave him a few rounds with the wrist rocket and he left. It wasn't a matter of hitting any vital part. You just sort of aimed for the bear.

A far more frightening incident occurred one night when Pat and I were working late in the old shop. It was a hundred feet or so from our little cabin, in an area that the bears used as a highway all night long. We'd left the kids with a babysitter, who foolishly went outside to talk to her boyfriend. Somehow Mike, who was just an infant, got out of his crib, opened the back door, and crawled through the night all the way to the back door of the shop, where we heard him trying to get in. That babysitter had a very short career with us.

I started the kids fishing when they were small, but I was careful not to start them too soon. If children aren't ready and don't have quite the patience, coordination, or enthusiasm needed to stick with fishing, you can ruin them forever by not waiting another year or two. They sense your frustration, and that can kill their interest.

I started them where my dad started me, on the Gallatin, with its quick little rainbows that weren't too choosy about lure or fly pattern. The most important thing for new fishermen, no matter what age, is action. You can show them the fine points any time, and if they're enthusiastic they'll pick them up themselves. But if they don't catch some fish and see the fun and excitement of it, all the lectures and instruction in the world won't help. At first the kids used spinning outfits because they're almost instantly easy, and they had a chance not only to catch fish, but to learn something about wading and reading the water. By the time they were ten or eleven, they switched to fly fishing, and they all loved it and still do. It got easier with each new child, too, because Greg took on a lot of the teaching himself, taking Mike and then Annette out fishing once he was old enough to go by himself.

When they were small I did a good bit of mulework, hauling one or two of them on my back across the water that was too deep for them. But very quickly they all had their own hip waders and were competent enough to get along. Annette was so small as a child, and only five feet two inches tall as an adult, that we had Marathon make a pair of custom waders for her. She wore them until she was about thirty, and she modeled them beautifully in our catalog. Waders often leak before you get them out of the box, but hers lasted forever.

It was also when the children were still small that we started teaching them to release their fish. This was before such practice was popular, and their friends used to look at them like they were crazy, but it was a good thing to teach them early. It seems to be something that is somehow harder for older people to learn. Greg, Mike, and Annette of course passed along their enthusiasm for preserving the trout in the stream to thousands of customers and clients, and the shop became our little forum for discussing trout conservation with the public.

Meanwhile, Pat generally took care of the money, and she was largely responsible for our success. She worked with the accountant, kept track of all the receipts, paid all the bills, and supervised all the help. She was always taking advantage of discounts, which often boosted our profits. We called her the shift boss. She set up all the shift schedules and assigned duties to people, made sure the shelves were always stocked and inventories were all up-to-date, and made sure that *nobody* stood around while working. Anytime anyone stood still, she'd find something for them to do, even if it was just to make sure no dust had settled anywhere.

That attitude kind of went against the old tradition of tackle shops, of course, which were usually somewhat gloomy little places where nobody would dream of dusting. There used to be a good-natured joke in the business that if you went into Dan Bailey's shop on a windy day, the dust would be so stirred up you couldn't even see Dan. Earlier generations of fishermen kind of liked it that way, and there isn't anything like the atmosphere in an old tackle shop, but we saw that fly fishing was changing, and new kinds of people, including more and more women, were getting interested. We knew that although the Trout Shop needed atmosphere, it needed a fairly clear one.

It was Pat who kept things running. I didn't have that kind of latitude to pay attention to all those things every day because people pretty much expected me to be available just to answer questions. I became the focal point for all the information that came in from the guides, the clients, the other customers, and various friends, so I was also the main distribution center for that same information. The way I saw it, they'd just prop me up somewhere and keep feeding me people with questions.

It was an interesting division of labor, and I know it's happened with other shop owners who get well known. People just insist on talking to that certain person they've heard of. It's important for business, too, because when the well-known person is in the shop, sales will often increase significantly. My family used to try to take the heat off me sometimes when people would start lining up to ask me questions, and eventually there were more and more people coming in looking for Greg, or Mike, or Annette specifically, but that took time. One day a fellow came in and waited very patiently while I worked my way through some other customers. It was late in the day, and I was just about worn out. Finally I got a minute so I could say, "I'm sorry, I'm just not going to be able to talk to you. Why don't you talk to my daughter?"

"Oh, no, I have to talk to you; everybody said I had to talk to Bud Lilly, and I want to get the straight dope."

"But she can help you as well as I can."

"Well, okay, but I'd really rather talk to you than that little girl."

I got busy again, and pretty soon he came over and tugged me on the arm, saying "Gosh, I'm glad I talked to her! She knows a *lot* more than you do!" I don't know, maybe she did. Annette's disadvantage was that she always looked like she was about fourteen years old, so I had to insist sometimes that "Either you talk to her or you don't talk to anybody." Once they talked to her for a minute, they realized she really did know fly fishing. She was sharp, she listened well, she was a good fisherman, and she was always up-to-date on what was going on in the area fishing. It was a good education for customers, especially the crusty old types who had never taken advice from a woman in their lives. Eventually there were a lot of people who would come in and say, "Where's that little girl? I want to talk to *her*."

When I started, I did all the guiding myself. Then I hired a guy from Connecticut, Chip Smith, and then I hired Al Troth. Greg started guiding when he was about sixteen, and by the time he was eighteen he was doing full-time guiding in the summer, which means that now, though he's not yet forty, he's got twenty years of experience on these western streams, and has floated many thousands of miles.

In the fall I'd have to go back to Bozeman to teach at the high school, but we'd keep the shop open, with Pat and Greg pretty much running things. Mike was still in high school and Annette was still in junior high school, but Greg was about to start his freshman year of college, so he was able to work later at the shop. I went up to West Yellowstone one weekend and Pat took me aside and said, "You know, Greg is getting awfully tired. He's been carrying a full load, and I think he's coming down with a cold. We'd better give him some time off. Besides that, he's about to start school, and he needs a couple days to rest up."

So I found Greg and said, "Greg, you're going to have to take some time off. You've guided for twenty-six straight days without a day off."

"Well," he said, "I'll take a day off if I can go fishing." So we gave him two days off so he could go fishing before he went back to school.

Both the boys started their guiding work as soon as school was out, the very next day, in fact. They both worked all their summers, paying for most of their college educations that way. Annette also worked like crazy all summer and at school, so none of the kids cost us much in education, and all were a great help with the shop. It made us proud and very happy to see our children not only taking part in the business, and not only succeeding, but sharing our love for the fly-fishing life. Both Greg and Mike developed reputations as superb guides, and as the Trout Shop got more publicity, so did they. Mike was the central figure in a story in Nick Lyons's book, *Bright Rivers*, and Greg was featured demonstrating fly casting in many photographs in Joe Bates's big book, *Fishing*. The boys and Annette became polished public speakers, giving many talks at fly-fishing meetings. They were our best spokesmen.

Annette was one of the first women in Montana to get a fishing outfitter's license. She took her first ladies-only trips, guiding women clients, when she was eighteen. Soon after that Greg's wife Bonnie began guiding too, which gave us an unusual edge on the shops with no women guides.

The year that Greg graduated, he and Barry Schaplow and Jim Ahrendes were all in the same class, but we couldn't give any of them time off to go to graduation; as soon as school was out, they all came up and went right to work. So the school mailed their diplomas to the Trout Shop. That night, when the boys came dragging in after dark from a long day of guiding, we waited until they were settled down by the fireplace before I announced, "All right, tonight we're having graduation exercises," and Pat and I presented them with their diplomas. They sat there kind of glassy-eyed, too tired to care one way or the other.

Greg and Bonnie got married that same summer. They had met at Montana State, where she was studying business education and was a basketball cheerleader. Bonnie was from Lewistown, Montana, so we had to arrange to get up there during the summer season for the wedding. Barry and Jim were in the wedding party. We left the shop in the care of Will Godfrey, who was working for us at that time, and the Lillys all took off for Lewistown.

There's a terrific spring creek that runs through Lewistown, and back in those days there were some enormous fish being taken from it. So the morning of the wedding, the boys decided there was just enough time for a little fishing. They pulled up in front of the church about ten minutes before the ceremony was to start, frantically trying to change out of their fishing clothes into their wedding clothes in the car. The wedding went just fine, and as Greg and Bonnie drove away on their honeymoon, Barry and Jim went back to the spring creek.

Mike met Karen at school at Pullman, and she worked a couple of summers at Mammoth in the Park. Mike would guide for twelve or fourteen hours a day, then drive forty-five miles to Mammoth, stay there half the night, and then drive back and guide the next day. After they were married, Mike decided he wanted to go to law school. So they went to Missoula, where he studied law and spent his summers guiding, which pretty much paid his way through school. Now he's doing very well in Bozeman, and we were proud to see him take part, as an attorney for the defense, in the famous "Mountain Man" trials in Virginia City (Dan and Don Nichols were tried for a kidnapping and murder committed near Big Sky in 1984).

Barry worked for us for several years, and eventually Pat, who noticed these things better than I, said, "You know, I think Barry has his eye on Annette." One summer he had to go to National Guard camp, and he was gone quite a while. When he came back for a visit, all the boys thought he'd come back to see the guides, but Pat said, "Nope—he came back to see Annette." She was right, as usual, and Barry and Annette eventually married. He earned his M.A. in wildlife management and went to work in Dillon, Montana, where they spent two years. Barry eventually let that job go and came to work at the Trout Shop full time. He was a trained fisheries biologist, and he gave the Trout Shop's credibility one more boost by being on the staff because he was also an excellent fisherman and guide.

When Annette was married, Pat decided that we would have a family get-together, and she wanted to serve fish. We had a kind of family policy that we didn't keep any fish, so whoever was the youngest member of the family was always the one required to kill fish if we wanted to eat some. It turned out that the youngest member of the family was Barry, Annette's new husband, so there he came sneaking in with six trout out of the Gallatin River.

We had some other family members that were an important part of our lives and of the Trout Shop. We've had several dogs, but none made the Trout Shop his territory so aggressively as Sam. Sam was a big black lab with a couple of unusual characteristics. One was that he loved rocks. If you took him to the river, he'd dive in and bring up a rock in his mouth. Some labs will do this sort of thing, but Sam eventually wore his teeth down so badly that in his later years he could hardly eat.

But what got Sam and us in the most trouble was that he loved Dairy Queen ice cream. The Dairy Queen in West Yellowstone was right across the street from the Trout Shop. Every day when the crowd would start to gather, Sam would stroll over to the Dairy Queen; whenever someone wasn't looking, he'd lose his ice cream cone. He was especially effective with small kids, who tended to gawk all around while they were eating and who, being short, held their ice cream cones just about at the level of Sam's nose. He had no mercy. Finally, the owner of the Dairy Queen called me up and said, "Bud, I know we're good friends and everything, but you're going to have to call that lab home. He's eating all my patrons' ice cream, and they complain, and then I have to replace whatever he ate."

So I apologized and promised to keep Sam home. For a while, every time he'd head across the street, one of us would holler at him to come back. We kept him in the shop a couple days that way, but then we got another call from Eileen over at the Dairy Queen.

"Bud, you still got Sam over there?"

"Yeah, we've been watching him."

"Let him come back. He keeps all the other dogs away."

Sam was a real fighter, and I suppose he was just keeping all the spoils for himself at the Dairy Queen. Eileen decided it was easier to deal with one Sam than with a whole pack of local dogs.

Sam ruled the Trout Shop the same way. Once in a while someone would make a mistake and bring their dog in. Then we'd have rods and reels and waders and things flying in every direction. When he got old and lost his ability to fight, he became more peaceable. One day a friend came in from Livingston and let his young lab out of his car. The dog came in and jumped on Sam and was just chewing the hell out of the poor old dog. This guy thought that was the funniest thing he'd ever seen, but I went over and kicked his dog about thirty feet out into the street, which ended the friendship. Sam was family.

This was during the years when we were boarding several of the guides in the shop basement. It wasn't the Ritz and had no ventilation, but it was cool, and Sam would go down there and spend the day. It smelled of old socks and Sam. I don't know how those guys stood it. They'd have to kick Sam out of someone's bed every night before they could go to sleep.

One February, when he was thirteen, Sam just went out and found himself a nice place under a tree and laid down and died. Greg found him in the morning.

By 1980 the Trout Shop was becoming less and less of a family business. Barry and Annette left to return to his family ranching business. They separated in 1984 and Annette went back to school in accounting. She's now working in that field in Alaska and doing very well. Mike was on his way to being an attorney when his marriage split up, he and Karen going their separate ways. Greg left in 1981, going to Seattle to study restaurant management at the University of Washington. As full as the Trout Shop still was every day, it seemed kind of empty.

Pat had been having health problems for a few years, and the long hours at the shop were pretty hard on her. So in 1982 we sold all the related businesses — the shop, the schools, the guide services, the catalog business, and so on — to Fred Terwilliger, a fellow Montana native who had worked for many years at Dan Bailey's shop. Things didn't work out for Fred, and in 1987 the shop passed into the hands of Jim Criner, former football coach at Boise State University. I will be working closely as a consultant with Jim, who is off to a good start with the shop, but I'm out of the shopkeeping business. It was an exciting, exhausting, and fulfilling thirty years, and I think my dad got his money's worth out of that original $2,500.

It seemed a little odd that there was no longer a Lilly in the tackle shop business. After all, it runs in the family. After a year in Seattle, Greg moved to Anaconda, where he invested in a photo processing service. He was working very hard at this, and making a big success of it. But the hours were getting to him, and he had never lost interest in an idea he'd discussed with me years before — opening a good tackle shop in Bozeman. In a little over a year he had doubled his investment in the photo business, so he sold out to his partner and came back to Bozeman. He got in touch with Dave and Lynn Corcoran, who had worked for me in West Yellowstone and who had since moved to Atlanta. They had always told Greg that if he ever decided to get back into the tackle business, they'd be interested in going in with him. So it was that the River's Edge opened in 1983, and it has been very successful. They're all working hard, running a beautiful and very classy shop, and spending a lot of their lives out on the streams. Now when I go fishing and get skunked, I go in and ask Greg what I was doing wrong.

4

CLIENTS AND
OTHER CHALLENGES

Among our guides who went on to open shops of their own was Will
Godfrey, who for many years ran a shop in Last Chance, Idaho on the
Henry's Fork.

Women clients appreciated the "Ladies-Only" trips with
Bonnie and Annette, an opportunity to learn fly fishing
away from male society.

Guiding the British Ambassador on the Lewis Channel,
Yellowstone Park, 1976.

The Ambassador's camp. Front row, left to right: Mrs. Townsley, Mrs. Ramsbotham, Sir Peter Ramsbotham. Second row, left to right: Greg, unidentified man, Bud, Yellowstone Park Maintenance Supervisor Bill Hape, Yellowstone Assistant Superintendent Bob Haraden, Superintendent John Townsley, Assistant Superintendent Vern Hennesey.

Where I grew up, if you wanted to fish, your father or a brother taught you, and you went fishing. I had no idea that there was more to it than that, so it took me awhile to get used to the idea that people would actually pay to be taken fishing. Pat Barnes was about the only really busy guide in West Yellowstone when I got there, and I could see that guiding was something we would have to do. During most of the 1950s I was the Trout Shop's only guide, just as Pat Barnes did practically all of his guiding himself. His wife Sig ran the shop while he was out, and my wife Pat did the same for us. I started out at twenty-five dollars a day, whether I was taking one fisherman or a dozen.

This book is as much about people as it is about fishing, and I suppose that's because in all those years of guiding, I was learning as much about my clients as I was about the fish. It's said that you don't really know a person until you've spent a couple days in the outdoors with him, and that proved true of guiding. We were learning all the time. I suspect our clients were, too.

Out here one of the things a guide simply has to know about is the salmonfly hatch. Salmonflies are the large stone-flies, some as much as two inches long, which appear on various western rivers in June and drive trout into the greatest surface-feeding binge of the year. It's a breathtaking event, and it's also the best time of the year to find really large trout — four pounds and up — willing to take a big dry fly. In the 1950s the few other guides were pretty secretive about it, and I was on my own. I had a couple from Texas who wanted to fish the salmonfly hatch, and I had little else going for me except that I knew a few stretches I liked to fish. So I took them down to an area I happened to enjoy, not knowing anything about the hatch.

We had an incredible day. I led them around just like I knew what I was doing, and we caught large browns until we were tired, including several that weighed over four pounds. When we quit for the day, we kept two, as was the custom then, and headed back to the car. As we crossed the road, some passing fishermen saw us dragging a couple of these big trout along. They swerved to a stop and ogled the fish while they asked us where we'd caught them.

"Oh, we just got them over there, in some good water."

"What on?"

"Salmonflies."

"My God, we just spent the entire day twenty-five miles down the river where the salmonflies are supposed to be, and we haven't gotten a thing."

What made that day stick in my mind wasn't the dumb luck of being in the right place at the right time. What was so memorable was that we caught only large fish. We caught lots of browns in the sixteen- to eighteen-inch range, plus the really big fish. We were probably ten miles upstream of the hatch, so apparently the fish had been feeding on the nymphs as they moved to shore and were really ready for the adults. Our big dry flies were just what they were waiting for, and there wasn't another fisherman for miles.

It seemed to me in those early years that some of my best triumphs as a guide were the ones I didn't deserve. When I was still new to guiding, a client insisted that I take him fishing on Hebgen Lake. Now, the routine ways to find fish in a lake are well known; springholes, inlets and outlets of creeks, weedbeds, and so on are all things a guide should look for. But this trip taught me about another one of nature's subtle signposts, the shoreline tire track.

We were trolling, not my idea of exciting fishing, but this man was a good friend and his mind was made up; Bud was going to take him fishing on the lake. When I finally got the motor started and we headed out, we worked along the shoreline until finally we started to catch fish. It seemed like a real hot spot, so I circled around back through the area a few times, and we caught fish each time. My client was really impressed, and I'm sure that part of my early reputation rested on just this sort of luck. What I noticed as we circled in the second time was that the bank was covered with tire tracks. The hatchery truck must have just left, and those poor rainbows were still bunched up trying to figure out where they were. My client didn't seem to notice that the fish were all exactly the same size.

After I got used to the idea of what I was supposed to do with a client, we were always looking for ways to find more of them, especially before the shop became well known. One of my brainstorms was to develop a partnership with a travel agent in an effort to keep a steady flow of customers coming in. I went to California and met with the travel director for Western Airlines. He was a fisherman, and we set up these "Western Tours," out of San Jose, that sold the fishermen a room at the Stagecoach Inn in West Yellowstone and some fishing with my guides. It sounded great.

I must have been insecure, because I set the price too low, drawing mostly non–fly fishermen: very nice people but hard on the guides. Our guides were hard-core fly fishermen, and when these Californians would come in with their little green canvas creels and their spinning rods, I could just see the guides cringing, hoping they wouldn't be called for this one.

This went on for an entire summer, and though any good guide is prepared to handle an occasional duffer, we got a new load of these guys with their salmon˙eggs and sinkers every few days. One group spent their first two days drinking and couldn't fish, so Barry took them horseback riding. I've never been more grateful to the guides for being creative and finding ways to get difficult clients into some good fishing. But it did bring a new phrase to the Trout Shop lexicon. Any time after that when a client arrived with all the earmarks of not knowing anything about fly fishing, I'd hear the guides mumbling, "Uh-oh — Western Tour."

Clients can be wonderfully generous at times. I was fishing with one client on the Madison when we saw the fish starting to work in the heavier riffles. I pointed them out to my client, whose name was Max, and he said, "I'm sorry, Bud, but I just can't wade out that far. Could you wade out and reach him?" So I waded out and put a fly over the fish, who took it and headed downstream a few hundred yards, where Max netted it for me. This was in the old days, so we hit it over the head; it was a four-and-three-quarter-pound brown. We went back upstream, and Max pointed out to the same riffle, saying, "Bud, I think there's another one out there."

"You want to try it this time?"

"Oh, no, I couldn't get out there."

So out I went again, cast the Sofa Pillow again, and took a near twin of the first trout. It took me back downstream where Max netted it, a four-and-a-half-pound brown trout.

These two fish were within ten feet of each other, and each was an outstanding trophy. Thanks to a client who just loved to see fish taken, I had the chance to take them within a few minutes of each other.

On the other hand, some people had some amazing ideas about what was appropriate to ask of the guide. About the time the West Yellowstone area began to get a lot of publicity in the 1970s, fly fishing became very fashionable, much the way skiing had some years earlier. It suddenly attracted a different crowd with a much higher percentage of urban people who knew practically nothing about the outdoors. There were many people who got into the sport almost overnight, and they wanted to move right to the top and not mess around with all the things the rest of us went through, like practicing and learning and getting experience. A surprising number of people came in and announced, "Now, we don't necessarily want to catch a lot of fish; we'd rather just have a few big ones." I think they really believed they were doing us a favor: Don't knock yourself out worrying about getting us the numbers, just put us on to a couple of those monster trout you have out here.

That's a fairly innocent mistake, of course. It's like the folks who would call up in January and ask me what the weather was going to be like during the third week of July, and if such and such a stream would be having good hatches right then. They didn't know enough to know what they didn't know. But other people simply had no sense of what was appropriate behavior when dealing with a professional guide, and even less sense about what was simply poor taste. One gentleman who had no shortage of money came into the shop one day and explained that he didn't really need a guide, that both he and his son were accomplished fly fishers. They even had their own rubber raft. But they would kind of like to know what stretch of water to fish, so would we mind if they followed one of the guides out to where he would put his boat in the water? They'd just put their raft in there and kind of drift along behind and not get in the way or anything.

There was another old gent who would hire a boat for the day. The man's son would put his raft in right behind the boat, and at lunchtime the father and son would trade places so that they had to pay the price of having only one person guided for the day.

What is curious about these incidents is that they almost always involved people for whom a little more expense would not have made any difference. They were willing to let their bad manners show in order to save a little money. In my experience, the guy who slaved and saved to make a float trip did all he could to have the full experience and didn't try to flimflam the guide or the outfitter. And those were the people we would work our tails off for, because they knew what it all was worth.

It's surprising, though, how many people would not follow the guide's guidance. There they were, paying $175 or more for the day of fishing with a guide who is presumably the person who knows most about the water they are going to fish that day. As I've explained, we spent a lot of time getting the best possible information on each stretch of water each day so that the guide would know what the best runs were, which flies to use, and so on. The guide wasn't just along to row. But many clients would refuse advice about the proper fly pattern, or the best places to cast, and sometimes they would ruin their chances by doing so. It's a shame to waste a good guide's knowledge that way, but people have their own notions of what to do.

But I must admit that there were times when we didn't

want the client to make *too* good use of the guide's knowledge. If we had reason to believe that the client might be a little too talkative about an especially good spot we'd shown him, we had some tricks for throwing him off. This was important if the client happily announced that he was going to bring his whole club back here tomorrow, and if "here" was some fragile place that couldn't take that kind of pressure. I think Greg developed the technique for getting the people turned around just enough so that they couldn't find their way back. If, for example, he was taking them somewhere on the Firehole (which is pretty much a roadside stream most of its length), Greg would drive past the turn he wanted to take, find some other road to turn onto, and make a loop back. Then he'd approach the important turn from the opposite direction. The Continental Divide runs right through the Park, and people are always getting confused with so many different watersheds so close together, so Greg's simple maneuver was usually enough to confuse them, even along a relatively short and highly visible river like the Firehole. This kind of maneuvering wasn't necessary very often, but with some fishermen it was our only choice.

But fly fishermen are generally wonderful people. We practically never had anyone make trouble, for example, over the inevitable slow day. There are days when you just can't buy a client a fish, even if the client is pretty skilled. In fact, we probably had more people get upset about a bad guide than about poor fishing. We would sometimes get a guide who either had a bad day or was an independent we had used because ours were all busy, and if he didn't perform well, people had a right to get upset. If the guide didn't give them a full day, or fished too much when he should have been helping the client, or in some other way didn't live up to the bargain, he truly had failed the clients, and I'd occasionally have to take it out of his pay.

People were reluctant to complain to me. They were trying to be realistic about fishing, I suppose, and keep in mind that nobody makes any guarantees that you'll catch fish. Some of them may have been embarrassed that they caught so few, which they should never be. Nobody catches them all the time, and nobody is testing them out there. They should just do their best and have fun. The last thing they should do is worry about what the guide thinks of their abilities; no matter how bad you are, he's seen worse, and his goal is to make the best of your abilities, whatever your skills or limitations.

The toughest guide trip we ever had was when we spent several days guiding a man who was totally blind. He insisted on fishing with flies, and he insisted on bringing his three children along and that they fly fish too. This was a very brave man who was determined that our guides could be brave too.

I sent two guides with him, and when they came in at the end of the day, the fly rods were tangled up in a hopeless rat's nest. It seemed like it took hours to get everything disentangled after those three nursery-school-age kids had spent the day with it.

The man could cast just fine, and so one guide, George Kelly, would get him into the stream and spot a fish, then tell him where to cast. As the casts got close, the guide would advise him, "about three feet farther," or, "a couple feet farther to your right," or whatever was necessary. Together they would zero in on the fish, and when the dry fly went right over it and it rose, the guide would yell "There!" and he'd set the hook. It was sad, and happy, and beautiful all at once.

In the meantime, the other guide was putting in a less fulfilling day, with three kids climbing all over him. Jim Ahrendes, a blocky, good-natured guy, got the assignment to watch over the kids, and he spent his day wrestling these kids up and down the river. One of them bit him, though Jim never did know why. Maybe the fishing was too slow.

*   *   *

It was inevitable that as the shop got better known we would begin to see some genuine celebrities coming in for a trip. Chet Huntley used to vacation up at the 320 Ranch north of West Yellowstone for some years before he got the idea for

Big Sky, the development he created between Bozeman and West Yellowstone. Chet was a native Montanan and a serious fisherman who usually came in August because he loved to fish hoppers. He got in the habit of stopping in the shop and became sort of a regular visitor. In fact, I believe it was Chet who introduced the Rappala to the West Yellowstone area. He came into the shop one day, I suppose it was in about 1965, and said, "I was over in Finland and they have this interesting lure — why don't you try it out?" He handed me this thing, and, not being much of a lure fisherman, I passed it along to a friend of mine who was a well-known fish-hog. He tried it out on Hebgen Lake and announced that it wouldn't work. Of course, eventually it became one of the most successful lures in the area.

It was through Chet that a number of other media personalities became our clients at the shop. Dan Rather was visiting Chet at Big Sky when Chet was just getting the development off the ground, and Dan and I fished together one day. We also got to know Robert Pierpont and Charles Kurrault through Chet.

You have to keep in mind that this was pretty heady stuff for a boy from Manhattan, Montana. I had a lot to learn about famous people and their world. Charles Kurrault used to stay at the Parade Rest Ranch near West Yellowstone, and one of his visits gave me a lesson in how peculiar fame can be. One day Ted Trueblood and Peter Barrett, both very well-known writers for *Field & Stream*, wanted me to take them fishing. Ted was one of the best known of all outdoor writers and an important conservationist down in Idaho, and I'd been reading his articles for many years. I really admired him, so I was just thrilled to take him and Peter fishing. Then at the last minute I got a request also to take Charles Kurrault out that day. That sounded like a pretty big deal to me too; how could I pass up a chance to fish with Charles Kurrault?

So I teamed them up when we met at the shop, going through the motions of introducing all these famous people to each other. But as I was making the introductions, I noticed the blank looks on all their faces as they shook hands. They all looked like perfect strangers look when they meet each other — polite and genial, but nothing more. It turned out that Charlie had never heard of Ted and Pete, and they had never heard of him. And there I stood, beside myself that I was taking all these household names fishing.

When I first fished with Charles Kurrault he was fairly new to fly fishing, but he has since become an avid Montana trout fisherman and seems to make a Montana visit almost every year. In the summer of 1986, Charlie was involved in the groundbreaking for the new wing of the Museum of the Rockies, and in his comments that day he mentioned that Montana trout fishing has become a regular thing for him.

One of the most serious fly fishermen among the celebrities we met at the Trout Shop was William Conrad, the great professional voice and star of the "Cannon" television show. Bill is an avid collector of fly rods and a very well-traveled angler; he's been featured on "The American Sportsman" series fishing in New Zealand, and it was my pleasure to take him fishing on the Firehole and the Madison in the Park. He returned to the area a number of times after that, and in fact, it was on a visit here that he met Tippy Huntley, Chet's widow, whom he eventually married.

Bill is a good sport as well as a good sportsman. He has been willing often to help out with good causes. In 1986, when I was working with the development corporation trying to promote the Bozeman area, I gave Bill a call and asked him if he would narrate a video we were putting together. Bill was glad to help out, as he so often has been with good causes, so our video will have that great voice of his carrying it along.

I suppose that of all the famous clients we've had, though, the one whose fishing style most suited my own is Curt Gowdy. Curt is an old-western-style fly fisherman, the kind who may not have classic form but who knows who to get results. He's a lifelong fisherman, a western native, and like many western fishermen I know, he's not a fancy caster or a hatch-matcher. But he understands the water and knows where to find fish. He's got a great deal of enthusiasm, and he's absolutely charming to be with, partly because his voice is so familiar. It's fascinating to hear that voice we've all heard for years on television sports broadcasts, except that now it's talking about fly patterns and trout.

Curt called me up one time and told me that the network was interested in making an episode of "The American Sportsman" around West Yellowstone. After explaining the plan to me, he asked, "Would you mind helping us out with this?"

"Why, Curt, I'd be delighted!"

"Great. Let's see, first, I need two helicopters, and . . . ."

"Uh, I don't know if I can arrange for two helicopters." Eventually the project fell through, and I still don't know how to arrange for helicopters.

Curt, Yellowstone's superintendent Jack Anderson, and I were fishing together in the Park one day, a tough one. Not only was the fishing slow, the wind was high. Jack was doing most of the guiding, so we were going to all his favorite places, and he also had brought along a fancy lunch. So in terms of everything but the trout — food, companionship, scenery — it was a great day. But we wanted some trout, too. There was a photographer following Curt around for something or other, and his day was a lot slower than ours.

Jack even brought along a bottle of "Old Yellowstone" bourbon, and he and Curt managed to just about finish that at lunchtime. Finally I suggested we try a spot I knew on the Firehole. When we got there, for some reason I suggested that we put a Bitch Creek nymph on the point, and then put another fly on the dropper. It was illegal to use a rig like that, with two flies, in the Park, but Jack didn't say a word. At the time, I didn't even think about it. I was just getting desperate to get some action from the trout, and this was a good technique.

Immediately Curt announced, around the big cigar he had in his mouth, that "By God, now we're doing it the way I learned to fish!" and we hoped that finally the photographer would get some action. Curt winged a good cast out and almost immediately hooked about a three-pound brown. It was a beautiful fish, and the cameraman was running up and down the bank trying to get a picture of this fish, which was jumping and putting on a great show before it finally broke off. It was the only fish we hooked all day, and the photographer never did get a decent picture of Curt with a trout. The interesting thing was that we'd spent the whole day doing the proper Firehole River sort of fishing, with small flies and hatch-matching and so forth, then finally went back to a basic old technique and hooked the only fish of the day.

I never considered Jack a client, even though we fished together a few times. We were sort of in the same business, dealing with the public, though he had a lot more pressure on him to produce than I did. He was superintendent of Yellowstone in the late 1960s and early 1970s, one of the most controversial periods in the Park's history. Though he's gone, he won't be forgotten by fishermen, because he set the Park on a management course that turned it into a world model of good fisheries management. That example has inspired good all over the country, and it was the best thing to happen in our area in many years — both for business and just for those of us who loved fishing.

I talked to Jack almost every Sunday. That was a fairly quiet day for him, and he'd drive down from his home at Park headquarters, at Mammoth Hot Springs. I think he liked that beautiful forty-five-mile drive early in the morning. He'd come in and we'd drink coffee and talk. Sunday morning was a quiet time in the Trout Shop, too, and it gave us both a chance to unwind a little. We'd swap stories, compare notes on fishing, and talk about the future of the area's natural resources. We supported his programs at the Trout Shop, and I like to think that we may even have had a little influence on his thinking. Fly fishing has had a lot of heroes, but few of them have done as much good for the actual fishing as Jack did.

One of my most memorable experiences with guiding a

prominent person occurred after Jack had retired and John
Townsley, now also deceased, was superintendent. John spent
a lot of time politicking on behalf of the Park by inviting
various dignitaries to visit, and it was because of one such visit
that Greg and I went into the headwaters of the Lewis River
in Yellowstone Park to guide the British Ambassador to the
United States, Sir Peter Ramsbotham. Sir Peter was, as you'd
expect, a gentleman in every sense of the word, and as this was
a specially arranged visit involving the State Department and
who knows how many other agencies and people, John wanted
to give the Ambassador a good chance to catch a trout. We
were pleased and honored to be asked to help out, and it was
really a lesson in how luxurious and well organized a camping
trip can be.

Sir Peter was an enthusiastic fisherman. He hadn't had
all that much experience with this kind of fishing, though, and
we happened to hit one of those periods in the late fall when
the fish in Lewis channel weren't easy to catch. Late fall is
when the spawning browns and lake trout move up to shallow
water, and sometimes they're thick and aggressive in the
channel. Almost any fly will take them. But this time they had
no regard for diplomatic standing, and the fishing was pretty
slow most of the days.

The Ambassador did hook one big trout. He hooked it in
the channel on a Montana nymph, and it was a good piece of
fishing because it was a bright day and the fish, like many
spawners, just weren't interested. They were spooky in that
shallow water and weren't showing much interest until after
sundown, when nobody was able to get good pictures. On the
first day, he caught several fish late in the evening, but the
action was so good and the light was so poor that nobody
thought to bother with pictures. The next day we were all set
to have a big day of catching fish, and it got very tough.
From that point on he only hooked the one big fish, which
got off after a brief fight.

The pressure was really on because they wanted to have a
fish fry, so Greg was fishing like crazy to accumulate enough

trout for a fish dinner for eight. He caught enough fish, but it wasn't as easy as wilderness fishing is advertised to be.

It couldn't have failed to be a great experience for everyone, though. John Townsley wasn't the kind of host who would take chances. The arrangements were made with military organization. Everything was always just so — the wood stacked just right, everything clean and perfectly organized. The food was superb. A helicopter had shuttled in everything, including a huge iron cookstove. We had fresh salads, all kinds of good things, throughout our four days there. The Ambassador and his wife were charming people; as so often happens when the fishing is slow, other parts of the outdoor experience — good cooking, good setting, and most of all, good company — take up the slack. And in a note to me afterwards, Sir Peter made sure I knew that he had enjoyed himself immensely, and he concluded by singing the praises of that wonderful fly I'd introduced him to, the "Manitoba Nymph."

There is one famous fly fisherman with whom I look forward to fishing some day, and that's Jimmy Carter. He fished the West Yellowstone area in 1981, having then just recently gotten interested in the sport, which is now apparently one of his favorite pastimes. We were able to persuade him to come and speak at the groundbreaking of the International Fly Fishing Center, which was a wonderful boost for publicity, and he did some fishing with Dave Whitlock and Charlie Brooks while he was there.

His fish and game director when he was governor of Georgia was a guy that I had gotten to know, and so the director had told him that if he ever got to West Yellowstone he had to go and see Bud Lilly. He was also a friend of a law family in Atlanta, Jack Izard, the oldest law firm in the south, and Jack also had told Jimmy the same thing — you gotta see ol' Bud Lilly.

I knew he was still in the area, and I had been warned that he might be dropping in on me, but it was still a little surprising when he did. It was early on a Sunday morning, probably the day he left the area. I'd opened the shop and it was still very quiet when I looked out and here was a parade of big black limousines surrounding the Trout Shop. People were piling out of them and running here and there, and a heavily armed guy came in the door — I was wondering by then if maybe the place was on fire — and walked up to me with a walkie-talkie in his hand.

"Are you Bud Lilly?"

"Yes." There was no denying it.

"President Carter would like to see you."

"Tell him to come on in."

So he came in, with some more guards, and we had a nice chat. Knowing that he was probably going to visit me, we had prepared a little presentation for him. I had a plaque made up with some flies and a peanut on it. There was a little inscription that said: "These flies are just like peanuts to the trout." We talked about fishing and mutual friends, and after he got back to Georgia he wrote me a nice letter telling me that he would like to go fishing with me next time he comes out. That would be just fine with me.

I did arrange for Jimmy to write the foreword for *Fly Fishing Always*, the little book published by the Federation of Fly Fishers in 1984. I called him up and told him that this was a good project, one that deserved the help, and he was more than glad to do it for us. He's a friend of fly fishermen and could help us in many ways if invited to do so.

Another friend of fly fishermen is a man I met just a few years ago, the great Olympic basketball coach from Indiana, Bobby Knight. Bobby has become an avid fly fisherman who has zeroed in on Montana fishing. He spoke at the International Fly Fishing Center, at our big banquet, a couple years ago, and he returns to the area regularly to fish.

Bobby is of course a very popular speaker in America today, an outspoken advocate of good sport and American values. I think he has great promise to be a good force for fly fishermen because he has such a large audience and such a commanding personality. I've fished with him a few times and intend to fish with him more; he's great company for his sense of good sport and his enthusiasm, and he's one of the great storytellers.

*   *   *

I'm still doing some guiding, but a lot of my guiding is for good causes. For the past couple of years I've had an arrangement with the International Fly Fishing Center by which I will guide for a day anyone who donates $250 or more to the Pat Lilly Art Gallery in the Center. There are several takers for that every year, and I've made similar arrangements on behalf of other good causes. Most recently, since I became a director of the Greater Yellowstone Coalition, that organization has been selling my guiding services for $1,000 a day, which is a far cry from what Pat Barnes and I were getting in 1951, even if I don't get to keep any of the money.

I enjoy it. I enjoy people, and I enjoy their excitement when they hook a good fish. Friends tell me that I'm an incurable guide, that when they go with me I'm just as likely to lead them around to good spots as I am to fish myself. It's a habit I don't really care to break.

5

EXPERTS

Don and Mary Martinez, probably about 1949.

Dave Whitlock, one of fly fishing's most versatile and inventive advocates, with more proof of his many talents.

Lefty Kreh and Pat in the shop.

Ernest Schwiebert, author of such important books as *Matching the Hatch*
and *Nymphs*, showing impeccable form as he lands a Firehole trout.
Ernie and I spent this day fishing and being photographed by
Dan Callaghan, one of fly fishing's best photographers.

At the 1974 FFF Conclave with Pres Tolman (left) and Arnold Gingrich.

Drawing a map for some friends at the head table at a FFF Banquet. From left to right, Yellowstone Superintendent Jack Anderson, Doug Swisher, Joan Wulff, Lee Wulff, and Bud.

Nothing is more uncertain or difficult to pin down in fly fishing than the notion of the expert. If you say the word "expert" to most fishermen, they immediately think of some person, either someone they know or someone they've heard of, who always seems to catch the big fish. If you say the same word to someone in the fishing tackle industry, they're liable to sneer and make a smart remark about "instant experts," or quote Lefty Kreh's comment that an expert is a guy with a slide projector, more than fifty miles from home.

Admitting right away that I wouldn't be writing books if at least a *few* people didn't consider me an expert, I have to say that the problem of sorting out the genuine authorities from the phonies is real. When the fishing around West Yellowstone started to get a lot of attention from the fishing writers in the late 1960s and early 1970s, those of us who lived there noticed a surprising increase in the size of fish being reported (but not seen or photographed) from some rivers.

I'd been keeping records in the Lunker Club book for many years, and I knew how rare a real three-pounder was. I knew that only once in a great while could the Firehole, for example, produce a fish in the six-pound class, probably only once every few years. We fished the rivers hard, and we measured and weighed those fish; the Trout Shop was the closest thing they had to an official record-keeper.

Then suddenly we started to read about four-, five-, and six-pounders being caught like fingerlings. I fished with some of those writers, and when there were witnesses around, the fish they caught looked pretty much like anyone else's, sometimes a little smaller. There was a lot of poetic license in those weight estimations, and there's no real harm in that except that it put those of us who ran tackle shops in an awkward position. People would come out having read so-and-so's book and expect to start hauling in the five-pounders from streams we knew had very few fish weighing over three pounds. We really knew, not only from our own experiences but from electroshocking studies that management agencies did.

So I'm sure I can't give you a simple definition of an

expert. It isn't just a guy who knows more than most of us. The late Ted Trueblood, for many years an editor for *Field & Stream*, was one of the first writers whose stories really stuck with me, but I don't think it was just because he obviously knew what he was talking about. Ted had a quality beyond expertise. Ed Zern, who has never pretended to be a great authority on anything, and whom I have always considered the greatest outdoor humorist, is also my idea of a real expert because he knows how to enjoy himself and his companions and good fishing and because he doesn't ever take himself too seriously. What expertise often is confused with, or replaced by, is the image of expertise. Consider, as I often have, something that seems very inconsequential at first but actually is very powerful. Consider the fishing hat.

People are pretty easily impressed once they get out of their own territory. We had a tackle shop owner in West Yellowstone for awhile who wore a western hat with a huge fleece hatband, the kind you could load down with flies. He had a real menagerie on that hat, and it became part of his trademark. People would come into the Trout Shop after they'd been visiting with this fellow, and they'd say, "Boy, that guy down the street, he knows a lot; he's got that terrific hat, you know, all full of flies . . . ." And I'd say, "Did he tell you about that hat?", acting innocent and honest.

"No," they said, all ears.

"Well," I'd wind up, "he was down on the Madison the other day and he fell in, and he got three strikes before he could get out."

I've thought about the hat for very good reasons myself, also having to do with image. I always wanted to popularize the western hat, partly because I was concerned about giving us a distinct image at the Trout Shop. I figured it was better than just wearing the Irish wool hats that have always been so popular among fly fishermen. So I started wearing my hat all the time, even in the shop. Some of those hats would get a lot of character over the years; I still have most of the ones I finally had to retire because distinctiveness was being replaced by seediness.

Well, it worked. The hat became a part of our image at the shop, I became very accustomed to wearing one, and people would sometimes look at me strangely if they saw me without it, like they weren't sure who I was. I didn't realize how successful I had been at developing the image until one day a fellow came into the shop and wanted to buy the hat right off my head.

"Jesus," he said, "I'd like to buy that hat. Is it for sale?"

"Everything is for sale in here except my wife."

"Well, I'd sure like to have that hat."

So I quoted him a price for it (there were a good many flies on it, as I recall), and he took it. I wore a western hat for twenty-five years in the store, though I finally had to quit because in the last few years I had a little trouble with skin cancers. I like to think that we had something to do with the popularization of western hats among fishermen and guides in our area, and I was glad to see it. I was glad partly because we sold Stetsons and Resistols in the shop, but also because it was part of the developing image of western fly fishermen. Easterners had their tyroleans and little tweed hats and all that, but there was no clearly identified western style.

The other hat that became closely identified with the shop was the one we'd advertise as "Greg's leather hat." When Greg and Bonnie were on their honeymoon in San Francisco, he found a wide-brimmed leather hat that had been made there. He came back wearing it, and I immediately announced we could make a fortune on that hat. We didn't really make a fortune, but we sold thousands of them over the years. I visited the factory once, down on Third Street, the same street where the Winston Rod Company was located for many years. It was a rough section of town, and Pat and I took a bus down to the address we had; there was the building with the windows all broken out, no sign, all boarded up. But the number was right, so I knocked on the door, and a little Chinese man peeked out. I asked him if this was the Winfield Cover Company.

"Yup."

"May we come in and look around? We're one of your customers."

"Okay." So we went in and I introduced myself. "I'm Bud Lilly from Montana."

"Oh, God, have we wanted to meet you! We've been wondering who those crazy people were in Montana who were buying all those hats!" There you have it. One man's expert was another man's sucker.

*   *   *

I was fortunate to start fly fishing with the help of an accomplished fisherman, my dad, and to grow up in a neighborhood where being a good fisherman was as natural as it could be. There were unlimited opportunities to fish, and experience really is one of the best teachers. I fished so much that I gradually came to recognize the good water in a stream without even consciously thinking about it. It's a slower way to learn than from books or professional guides, but what you learn you learn very well. I came to the Trout Shop with a lot of fishing experience for someone my age, and enough sense to know that I had a lot more to learn. Luckily for me, the Trout Shop was a great place to do that learning.

They stopped planting fish in the Park by the late 1950s. They recognized that it was a mistake, even before studies were done which proved that stocked fish can hurt the native fish population. But back when they were still stocking Park streams, they used to plant big rainbows from the Ennis Hatchery in the Firehole and Madison rivers. In the early 1950s we kept track of that, and we knew about when and where they would be putting those fish.

One day I took a retired army man, whom we knew as Colonel Frierson, to the Firehole. He had been after me to take him fishing, and I didn't tell him what I knew about the hatchery truck schedule. The Colonel was a proper fisherman, with the best tackle and skills in delicate presentation, but I was just sloppy enough that I could catch those hatchery fish, while the Colonel just couldn't catch a thing. I had taken Greg along, who was about five years old at the time, and as soon as we walked back into the shop he announced to all the people gathered there that "Daddy caught some, but Colonel Frierson didn't catch any."

But I learned a lot from clients and friends like the Colonel. My background in Montana trout fishing was pretty narrow, and I was grateful to these men who came from other parts of the country with all kinds of new ideas and techniques.

I learned a lot from a man named Irving Strong. Irving was an excellent fly fisherman, though I got the impression he was one of those people who had been put out to pasture by a wealthy family back East. Irving really taught me most of the fundamentals of dry-fly fishing. I knew nothing about how to pick a fly off the water with a roll cast. Irving knew a lot about how to read rises, how to tell a caddisfly rise from other kinds, for example.

The first fishing book that had any effect on me was Ray Bergman's *Trout*, the book that so many fishermen still consider their Bible. Bergman fished the Yellowstone country and wrote about it in *Trout*, including telling about fishing with Vint Johnson, one of my early competitors in West Yellowstone. Vint Johnson had shown Bergman how effective a big Royal Coachman bucktail was on trout in the Park, and after reading that, I began to promote not only that fly but a number of other bucktail and squirrel tail patterns.

Sid Gordon's book *How to Fish from Top to Bottom* had a big influence on me. It contains so much information on the character of streams and lakes, and how fish go about their lives, that I still recommend it to people all the time. What he did was reveal to me how important it was to be aware of the conditions on any given day. Having all the famous fly patterns and knowing a lot of fancy casts wouldn't really do you much good if you didn't understand the influences of sunshine, water temperature, air temperature, shade, and other factors on the fish and their world. I still find it best to concentrate more attention on those conditions rather than on having a fly with just the right shade of hackle in the tail. By spending many years observing those environmental conditions, I got a reputation for being able to predict fishing conditions.

I noticed, for example, a correlation between the catch-rate of spawning brown trout in the fall, and barometric pressure. Our experience showed us that on a day with a fast-falling barometer, brown trout would be much harder to take. We had some theories about why this happened, but it was a priceless piece of information for guides and fishermen, and we earned it the hard way, by watching and keeping track of how the fishing went in relation to all these environmental factors. We got so we watched the barometer in our shop every day.

I suppose the reason we got so sensitive to these environmental conditions was that we were right on the edge of Yellowstone Park, where there is a unique range of such conditions in trout streams very close together. The Firehole, Gibbon, and Gardner rivers all have significant geothermal influences that dramatically affect their fishing, and they flow into larger streams that also are influenced. There's no place else in the world where you have trout streams of such ecological diversity so close together. If you know the streams, and are aware of how environmental conditions are influencing them, you can almost always find at least one place where the fishing is promising.

I always have loved streamer fishing, but I think it was Joe Brooks who really popularized the big western streamers. Joe was a good friend of Dan Bailey's and he didn't spend much time in the West Yellowstone area. He used to stay in a cabin right on Nelson Spring Creek south of Livingston, back before anybody had heard much about the tremendous fishing in the spring creeks. He and Dan started using really large streamers, larger than those to which trout fishermen were accustomed. Joe often used his famous series of "Blondes" (saltwater flies five or six inches long) on a shooting head, and he took some enormous trout from the Yellowstone with them. It didn't take long for me to get interested in that, and since then I've always been a believer in very large streamers. Now, what with the books of Joe Bates and Sam Slaymaker, there's no shortage of information on streamers, and there are a huge number of good patterns. But for the really large trout, especially the big browns on their fall spawning runs, you can still do very well with the big Blondes developed by Joe Brooks.

Before I got to know any of the really famous fishing experts, I naturally got to know some of the behind-the-scenes people who have a great deal to do with the success of the experts. I had the pleasure of meeting many of the leaders in the industry, often just when they were getting started. We were able to work with Leon Martuch, Sr., when he was getting Scientific Anglers started. Leon had involved Ted Trueblood in his company, and Ted was a creative guy who deserves a lot of credit for some of the Scientific Anglers projects. I know he was very involved in the development of the first sinktip lines. I didn't really see good fly rods in any appreciable number until Paul Young came out from Detroit in about 1955 looking for someone to open a dealership. He called on Dan Bailey, who for some reason either made Paul angry or offended him, and so Paul approached me. I was delighted to carry the rods. Paul Young built beautiful rods that were great fishing tools, and I still use a couple Young rods now and then for fishing smaller waters.

Of course, one of the modern western fly-fishing masters was Dan Bailey, who always will be remembered not only for his many contributions to fly fishing, but also as one of trout fishing's staunchest conservationists. Dan and I were competitors, but we often found ourselves next to one another in some battle to protect the streams from some idiotic dam or diversion project. This was an endless fight, and Dan had started fighting it virtually alone, well before the rest of us got involved and a system of fishermen's organizations was developed.

In 1986 Charlie Waterman published a fine book about Dan, called *Mist on the River*, and I can't think of anyone more deserving of Charlie's skillful attention than Dan. Most fly fishermen who remember him know all he did for western fly fishing — helping develop the Wulff flies, popularizing the modern version of the Muddler Minnow, and much more — but they should remember him also as one of the original western trout crusaders. His son John still runs the shop in Livingston, with Red Monical, and they have established a memorial award in honor of Dan, given every year to some deserving conservationist or group.

One of the first of the present-day fishing writers whom I got to know was Ed Zern. I first took Ed fishing in July of 1963. There were four of us, including Sam Radan, Ray Rhoades, Ed, and me, and for some reason I was using a big eight-man Air Force surplus raft. I was not known as an expert in raft management and for some reason had brought along only one paddle rather than the customary two oars, so Ed and the others spent much of the day fending us off banks as I furiously switched the paddle from one side to the other. He had just returned from Scotland, where his hosts had presented him with a beautiful hardwood wading staff with a staghorn handle and a brass ferrule on the end. He was a great sport about the extra duties, but eventually he poked this gorgeous wading staff into a bunch of willows that kept it, and I had to pile out of the raft and fight my way back upstream through the brush to retrieve it.

The salmonflies were on that day, and the fishing was outstanding. Ed had never caught a brown over eighteen inches long in all his years of fishing, and as this was his first trip to the Madison, he was probably unprepared for the kind of day you could have during the salmonfly hatch. We put in at Varney Bridge and, thanks as much to the others keeping us out in the current as to me paddling like mad, we found our way to a good run where we could see trout rising. We beached the raft, started casting, and immediately were all into big fish. Ed hooked a twenty-inch brown that he landed after ten minutes of jumping and running (by both Ed and the trout), Sam took a twenty-one-inch rainbow, I took a twenty-two-and-a-half-inch rainbow, and Ray lost a fish bigger than any of ours. It was like that all day. We caught several fish weighing over three pounds, and I caught a rainbow that weighed five pounds two ounces. Ed caught one rainbow over four pounds that we photographed and released, the largest rainbow he'd caught in his life up to that point.

A few years later, in 1968, when I was putting together my first catalog, I asked Ed if he would write a little foreword and let us use the photograph of him with the big rainbow. He immediately agreed, but he had a sad story to tell about the photograph, a story he related in his foreword:

> Writing forewords to somebody else's book is a chore I usually avoid, but I volunteered for this one. Not because it's likely to win a Pulitzer Prize, but because Bud Lilly is a guy I've known since before I was senile, for whose knowledge of Western fishing and of proper tackle for it I have immense respect, and whose skills as a trout man I envy and admire.
>
> Also, there's the fact that one of the photos that should be in this book, perhaps even on the cover, isn't there. I took it one day just after I had beached just under four pounds of wild brown trout that had taken a fly Bud had given me a few hours earlier, and while I was admiring it Bud came whooping down the river with a rainbow of just over five pounds on the other end of his line. When he had netted it and brought it ashore and weighed it I broke out a Pentax camera and spent ten minutes photographing Bud with that picture-book rainbow. Then, dammit, I lost that roll of film, and even today have hopes of finding it in an old fishing-jacket pocket or some dark corner of my tackle box (on the same roll I had my only photos of the largest brown trout I had ever caught). So in a way, this is a poor substitute for a photo that might have said more about Bud and his expertise than any mere words can do.
>
> Buying tackle from a catalog, of course, isn't as good as buying it from Bud's store in West Yellowstone, where you can paw through flies and lines and reels to your heart's content, and watch a lot of famous fishermen come by to pick up oddments of tackle or the latest dope on the fly hatches or just to gab a bit with Bud. But a lot of us live a long way from the Trout Shop, and this is the next best thing to actually being there, leaning on a counter and arguing about the proper monstrosity to imitate a natural salmon fly. So until we meet there in person, good fishing.
>
> Ed Zern

Besides his good sportsmanship and sense of humor, Ed was a great fishing companion because of his ability to tell a story. On that trip he told a story that went on for an hour or so while we were fishing, about his experience at a restaurant in Three Forks; the whole thing was fiction, made up as he went along, and it flowed as smoothly and entertainingly as if he'd spent weeks writing and rewriting it. Ed Zern is a very creative man.

My business gave me the opportunity to meet and help some of the best fly tiers in the world. We helped develop the careers of some superb new talents, and allowed some well-known talents to broaden their audience and market. Dave Whitlock, Al Troth, and Jack Gartside, all enormously talented guys, got their commercial start through the shop. It was a matter of importance to us that besides the full selection of flies tied by professional tiers who were more or less anonymous, we offered many specialties — flies by Darwin Atkins, George Grant, Rene Harrop, and others. It was an exciting time for us, keeping in touch with these highly creative individuals, seeing what they developed, and testing some wonderful new fly patterns just as they first appeared from the vises of their creators.

We did the same thing with blossoming artists. The Gallery introduced us to many fine young artists who needed a boost. We never took credit for their success — if they hadn't been good artists, it wouldn't have mattered how much we promoted them — but we did feel good about helping them while at the same time helping our business.

Dave Whitlock had gotten started as a commercial fly tier in the Oklahoma–Arkansas area, but I was pleased to help him get started in the West. He came to my shop in the late 1960s with some of his flies, and they were extremely impressive. When our first catalog appeared in 1969, I had three pages of Dave's flies. We continued to offer them, and he kept coming up with new ones. We were sure from the start that this man was going to be an extraordinary influence on fly fishing, and he has been. I'm not sure anyone has influenced fly tying since World War II more than Dave. He has become one of the most adept public speakers on fly fishing, he's published some excellent, practical books, he's championed his well-known Whitlock–Vibert box for stocking trout eggs in streams, and, more than practically any of the other modern authorities, he is versatile. He's a great all-around fisherman, able to do well with anything from the smallest nymphs to the largest streamers (his Multi-colored Marabou Muddlers are among the most important new streamers since the Muddler itself appeared forty years ago), he has adapted fly fishing to many species of fish not usually taken on flies, and he's the kind of sportsman who is never too busy to help another fisherman.

Until the last fifteen or so years, we didn't have any nationally known fishing writers who specialized in the Yellowstone country. There were various local guidebooks now and then, and there was an occasional little book published by some fisherman from another part of the country. Howard Back's beautifully written little book, *The Waters of Yellowstone with Rod and Fly*, published back in the 1930s, was about the most you would find about this area unless you collected the articles in outdoor magazines for years until you had a good file. But part of the boom in publishing in the 1970s was the appearance of more local writers, and I'm sure none of them have been more closely identified with our area, or have been more successful in writing books about it, than has Charlie Brooks. After his first book, *Larger Trout for the Western Fly Fisherman*, appeared in 1970, Charlie became the leading fly-fishing writer of this area. It's been an interesting change from the old days, when only outsiders wrote about our fishing, and even though Charlie died in 1987 after a long fight with cancer, his influence will last many years.

Books sometimes have funny effects that you wouldn't expect. When Charlie started publishing his very popular books, he moved into a vacant niche in fishing writing. There was nobody really paying full-time attention to the big weighted flies, and Charlie was a great proponent of those flies. He had the strength of his convictions to carry the principle of the weighted fly to a logical conclusion, and one reason his flies work so well is that he wasn't shy about making them heavy enough to reach the fish. In a way he was challenging traditional perspectives, and he took some criticism for promoting flies that are as heavy as lures. Those of us who use the heavy flies believe we're not doing anything unsporting, and Charlie did a lot to give those flies more credibility.

On the other hand, his books tended to create fishermen who believed they could learn it all by just reading a book. There was something about Charlie's way of writing that seemed to bring that out in people. As much as he encouraged people to do their own studying of streams, and to think for themselves, the biggest effect I saw of his books was that crowds of people would show up at certain spots, just as the books told them to, and expect to catch big fish almost automatically. People went through his books page by page, and more or less thought that that was all that was necessary. Charlie talked a lot about the Barns Pools, a series of runs on the Madison just a few miles upstream from the Park boundary. These pools are great for migrating trout that move out of Hebgen Lake to spawn in the late fall, and Charlie told of his exploits with those fish. All summer long people would come into the shop and complain that they couldn't catch those fish that Charlie claimed were in those pools, and I'd have to explain that the fish weren't there yet, that the fishing only got good in October.

Charlie's books generated a lot of enthusiasm for fishing in our area, and he earned a lot of credit for that. He was an avid conservationist and always stressed releasing fish. But he was also the most controversial fishing writer the Rockies has produced. Many people I know out here felt that their confidence had been betrayed when his books included information they had given him, because they'd worked hard to learn things about the local fishing that they didn't necessarily want published. One fellow came into the shop shortly after Charlie's book *The Trout and the Stream* came out and said, "I think I'll buy six copies and burn 'em." That's a lot of hostility for a fishing writer to generate.

The most frequent complaint I heard at the shop about his books was that they ruined this spot or that spot by exposing the good fishing in a specific pool or stretch of water. It was Charlie's right to publish what he wanted, of course, and the Trout Shop sold hundreds of his books and thousands of his flies, but my own approach to telling people about fishing has gone exactly in the opposite direction. In my other book, *Bud Lilly's Guide to Western Fly Fishing*, I stress being aware of the season and all the related conditions, knowing a good bit about the tackle, and going out and finding your own fishing rather than catching someone else's trout. Over the the years we've had to get away from telling people exactly where to go and behind which rock to cast. But that's not the way Charlie saw it, so we just agreed to disagree. I'm sure that some of the people we guided over the years at the Trout Shop went out and revealed good spots we'd shown them; anyone who guides shares some responsibility for spreading the word about a good fishing spot. The difference between Charlie and me is that my approach is to try to spread that use around, letting it move with the seasons and changing conditions, while Charlie's approach, whether intentionally or not, tends to concentrate fishermen in a few spots.

The nice thing is that the rivers themselves will eventually make a lot of this debate academic. Anything you publish will start to be wrong almost immediately as the river changes its channel, as the silt moves around, and as the fish subsequently find new lies. The more specific a book, the shorter its useful lifespan. The really important things about Charlie's books, such as his introductions to stream ecology and his recommendations on fly patterns, will be useful for a long, long time.

Charlie's books were part of that great surge of fishing book publishing in the 1970s that brought so many new names to the attention of fishermen and that brought some of the old masters back into print. The various seminars and trips we arranged at the Trout Shop gave me a chance to meet some of these very talented people, and others I met through the

Federation of Fly Fishers, which started holding its annual conclave in West Yellowstone every year or two in the late 1960s. This was an especially important experience for me; no matter how good you think you are at something, you can always learn by watching someone else, whether that person is just as good or better.

Ernie Schwiebert was one of the great fishermen I met in the 1960s just before we started developing our various special seminars, and Ernie is really an exceptional fisherman, a classic in his style. He follows all the proper procedures, all the good manners, and he's had a very broad experience that has taught him more than most people will ever have a chance to learn. Fishing for giant salmon in Norway, big brook trout in Argentina, and many kinds of fish elsewhere has turned Ernie into a great angler.

He's not an early starter. The first big challenge is to get him out of bed. If you're going to fish with Ernie, we learned, you start your day around twelve or one o'clock because Ernie likes to stay up late and celebrate the previous day's successes.

Ernie isn't a fisherman for the brawling, stony, big rivers. His special interest is in streams, where he can practice his wonderful skills with aquatic entomology and delicate presentation. We took him floating on the Madison a couple of times, and he didn't really enjoy it much. He prefers rivers like the Firehole and the Henry's Fork.

And there is no question that of all the people with whom I've fished, none of them could identify what difficult fish are feeding on and match it any quicker than Ernie can. He is a master. He's also a master at using emergers. I've watched him make extraordinarily long casts, straight across the Madison in the Park, using extremely long leaders in the eighteen-foot range, and take large browns on #20 emergers. He is an excellent caster, accomplished at handling a line in tricky currents and fishing a dry fly in any direction, upstream or downstream.

Once in late June I brought Ernie in to conduct one of his afternoon clinics for us. We had some free time, so Annette and I took him into the Park to fish the Madison and the Firehole. As we were driving along the Madison, I spotted a big trout rising right up against the near bank, so we pulled over and I put Ernie onto the fish. Ernie got his tackle strung up and was just working into position to cast to this brown, which must have been eighteen inches long, when up pulled these three motorcycles. Three big guys with leather and beards and bellies got off and started strolling over toward the river. Without even thinking, I reacted by calling to them.

"Wait a minute, wait a minute! You're going to spook our trout!"

These three big hulks looked over at me, and one of them said, "Whaddya mean, spook yer trout! This here's a state park and we can do whatever we want." That quickly they had demoted Yellowstone from a national to a state park, redefined good manners on public land, and scared the devil out of Ernie's trout. But Ernie, who had served on a special advisory committee for the Secretary of the Interior as a fisheries expert, really enjoyed the part about the state park.

Ernie is so well known on trout streams that people often recognize him, which must get tiring sometimes. One day Ernie and Dan Callaghan, who is an outstanding fly-fishing photographer, and I were fishing the Madison in the Park, a section right along the highway. I saw these people pull over into the parking area and watch us for awhile, and I figured Ernie's notoriety was catching up with him again. Finally they came over closer to us, walked right past Ernie, looked at me, and said, "Oh, you're Bud Lilly!" Ernie enjoyed that, too.

Ernie has been in the enviable position of fishing everywhere in the world and getting paid for it. Shortly after his first visit to the shop in 1965, I wrote to thank him for the publicity a story of his had given us. His response was a quick glimpse into what life was like for fly fishing's other half:

Dear Bud:

Am pleased the Firehole story brought you some business, and that some of the people I personally sent your way actually showed in West Yellowstone. You have a fine shop and deserve the business, so no thanks is necessary.

Have been to Argentina since I last saw you. Best fish were a 16 pound brown, 18 pound landlock, 12 pound rainbow, and 9 pound brook. This winter I have been busy here, so am only thinking about it unhappily! Last July I fished salmon in Norway and killed a 51 pound fish with a 9½ foot Young Parabolic, WetCel Wf-11-S High Density, Hardy St. Andrews, 12 pound tippet and 2/0 Dusty Miller. Once in a lifetime!

Sorry to miss your fishing in past months, because I really love early fall in the Rockies.

Cordially,
Ernie

Among the leaders of the new generation of scientific anglers that appeared in the late 1960s were Doug Swisher and Carl Richards. We announced the forthcoming publication of their book, *Selective Trout*, in our 1970 catalog, with a few of their remarkable photographs of mayflies and a picture of Doug and Carl. They are among the outstanding modern trout-fishing technicians, of course, and we involved them in some of our special seminars. They were both good at sharing the knowledge that made *Selective Trout* such a bestseller, and eventually Doug set up a school of his own in Darby, Montana.

Some of what I thought of as the most characteristically *western* fishing didn't interest them, though. They weren't interested in fishing the fast, turbulent streams, the sort of water where the whitefish have to hold hands. They were specialists in accurate identification and imitation of stream insects, and the way I learned to fish, with general fly patterns that served lots of purposes, wasn't like that.

I fished with Doug and Carl down on the Henry's Fork one day during one of our clinics. The fishing was terribly difficult and nobody was doing well, which always looks a little embarrassing for the experts. After awhile we spread out and lost sight of each other, and when we joined up again Doug made a remark that was destined to add another expression to the sarcastic lexicon of the Trout Shop guides. He reported that he'd caught and released a good one, "over on the other side of that island." My guides latched on to that and soon were talking about "island fish," those being the ones that nobody else saw and that were always several inches bigger than anything anyone else caught that day.

For all the good that Doug and Carl did with *Selective Trout*, I think that in the long run their most important contribution to fly fishing will not be their no-hackle flies or any of their other developments. Those things have been accepted by a lot of people, but I think more important is that Doug and Carl have made us all think about things we took for granted and have shown us the importance of experimenting. Those beautifully clear photographs of trout-stream insects opened a window for us onto a world about which we really didn't know much.

Hatch-matching theory is of course one of the biggest topics in fly fishing. It's amazing how determined some fishermen will get in defending a certain hypothesis or approach to fly patterns. I do know that there are times when having the right fly is terribly important; I've been skunked often enough by very difficult fish to understand that sometimes you have to pay close attention to fly choice. But the quest for the "only good fly" has a tendency to get out of hand. When I was still running my shop in West Yellowstone, I got in the habit of keeping track of these good flies.

For example, let's say there was a very good day on the Firehole River, with lots of fishermen out there. Over the course of the day I might have talked to fifty or more fishermen, all of whom wanted to come back and tell me about their success.

"How was the fishing?"

"Oh, God, it was fabulous, fabulous!"

"Was it tough, or easy?"

"Oh, they were selective, very selective."

"What were you using?"

"*The only thing they would take* was this little beauty here . . . ."

Of course, by the end of the day I'd seen about fifty different "only things." I went through this time after time.

I should have developed a series of flies called the Only Things.

There is a lot to getting the right fly and presenting it well. Presentation is written about too little, compared with fly-pattern theory. Does the fly have any action, or does it accidentally work across the current? Is the tippet small enough to avoid influencing the fly's motion? Is the size of the fly right? There are lots of things that are important besides fly pattern, and even having a proven pattern isn't always good enough if your particular samples of that pattern are poorly tied. For example, it's very hard to get a good Joe's Hopper now, and bad ones are almost worse than worthless. There's no shortage of things to worry about when you're trying to take a fish on a fly. We shouldn't concentrate on just one of them, especially when it's the one that is the most susceptible of all to changing fashions. New flies come and go like weather, but if the fisherman knows how to read the stream and handle the fly rod, he can do well with relatively few patterns, most of which have been around a long time. After all, this is the West, you know; our fishing may be getting harder, but it hasn't been that many years ago that Dave Bascom was catching trout on Yellowstone Lake with a lure made from a beer-can opener.

Lee Wulff is a good example of a fisherman who knows the basics so well that he can do well under difficult circumstances. Lee is, of course, one of the best-known anglers of this century, and I was able to fish with him, and Joan, a few times. Lee is a marvelous fisherman in that he knows where the fish are likely to be in the stream; he is superb at reading water. He also knows that if he gives the fish the right impression in a fly, he doesn't have to worry about exact imitation; the superior fish-catching qualities of his Wulff series of dry flies, my favorite being the Royal Wulff, prove his point.

Lee has always been known as a very athletic fisherman, catching an Atlantic salmon by casting for it by hand and playing the fish with only a reel and no rod, and other equally impressive tricks. What was surprising to me, and I think it should be instructive to all of us, is that his casting presentation is pretty rough. It made mine look deluxe. But he caught fish.

I fished with him on the Firehole one August, a stream and a time that will test anyone's skill. As usual Lee was trying out some new patterns, this time some plastic-bodied grasshoppers he was getting ready to market. He was very lackadaisical about his presentation. Like me, he didn't go in for the modern fly fisherman's fashionable crouch (the famous Henry's Fork Hunchback), but he didn't make much effort to cast nicely, either. He just sort of slapped it out there, which often is the best way to fish grasshoppers anyway, and he was picking up fish regularly.

It's interesting to contrast these great fishermen sometimes. For example, we had Ed Shenk out one summer doing a clinic for us. Ed is almost a legend in Pennsylvania for his ability to take large trout on flies, and he is of course best known nationally for developing some excellent fly patterns, especially terrestrials. We took him into the Park one hot August day, the hardest time of the season to get Firehole trout to take, and he put on a show of precise, careful casting that his clinic group will probably never forget.

Ed was using one of his little six-foot bamboo rods, and he worked up the river, popping a little Letort Hopper right against the bank, taking fish after fish. His approach was different from Lee's, or mine, or other good fishermen I know, but it worked beautifully. There are lots of ways to catch a trout. Maybe that's why there are so many experts.

Ed was also one of the most talented fly tiers who visited us. I think that even with all the modern developments coming out of the West, from the great younger fly tiers on the Henry's Fork to the various spring creek authorities, the seat of much of the fly-tying talent and innovation is still in the East. If they want to catch fish on those hard-fished streams, they simply have to be smart, and they have to come up with fly patterns that are reliable. When you get only one chance, you have to make it count. That may be why for so many years western fishermen were less concerned about fly pattern and presentation. They could usually find plenty of fish. As Lefty Kreh put it one day on the Madison when the big rainbows were hitting fast, "These fish are like streetcars — if you miss one, there'll be another one along in a couple minutes."

Certainly one of the most serious students of fly-fishing theory whom I ever met was Vincent Marinaro, author of one of the great modern fishing books, *A Modern Dry Fly Code*. Vince came out one summer in the late 1960s before the Federation of Fly Fishers conclave, and he stayed with Pat and me. The Federation officers asked me if I would take him around the area and show him some of the streams. We got ready to go fishing in the morning, and I was loading my gear in the car when I noticed that Vince didn't seem to be bringing along a rod or anything. I asked him, "Aren't you bringing any tackle?"

He said, "No, I want a rake and a bucket."

"Don't you want to fish?"

"No, I just want to take a look at all the insects."

So we went out to Thompson Spring Creek, one of the fine little creeks in the Gallatin Valley near Belgrade, where he collected insects to his heart's content. He had heard of Thompson, and he made a comment about it that I have heard others make — that it really reminded him of his Pennsylvania streams, especially the Letort.

Then we went home and he discussed insects until three o'clock in the morning. He really liked to talk, and I must have been a good listener.

On the opposite end of the spectrum are the nontheorists, people like Nick Lyons and the late Arnold Gingrich, who bring the best of fly fishing's other side — the warmth, the fraternity, the foolishness — to life for us. Arnold was master of ceremonies at several FFF conclaves in the 1970s, and he was truly a master. He was so articulate and well-read that he could synthesize and coordinate and review and summarize and placate and bullshit, and he loved being associated with the great fly fishermen. I think fishing was his idea of a great vacation from his other work, and he portrayed the brotherhood of fly fishing beautifully. I enjoyed being in any party of which he was a member because the banter was several levels above what we usually encountered in West Yellowstone.

Arnold came out to a conclave in West Yellowstone just a year or two before his death. He wasn't in great health, so we went to some fairly quiet water on the Firehole. Arnold was devoted to very small rods, and so he spent most of his time untangling the fly from the grassy banks behind him. That was the last time I saw him, and fly fishing lost one its best friends when he died.

Arnold was a central part of a very exciting period for fly fishing, and it was exciting partly because we were discovering all these experts, who were almost like heroes to the average fly fishermen. Fly fishing has probably never had a more satisfying social life. One of the early Federation of Fly Fishers conclaves in West Yellowstone was held before they would allow liquor at the Convention Center, and so I hosted a cocktail party in the Trout Shop. I invited about one hundred and fifty people, and the night of the big dinner we closed early, about six o'clock. We set up a bar, and I had Mike and Greg and Annette and all the guides packing drinks and peanuts to everybody. Arnold had a few martinis and settled into a comfortable spot on the stairway, where he signed books and held forth on many subjects. Ernie Schwiebert and all the others were there, talking and drinking and having a big time; the atmosphere of the Trout Shop, with all the tackle and outdoor clothes and art surrounding the people, seemed just perfect for this kind of get-together. We were having so much fun that we forgot all about dinner. Finally, they called us from the Convention Center and said, "Would you please close down the party so we can get everyone back here and serve them dinner?" For me, times like that were when fly fishing's experts were at their best.

*   *   *

When I think back on half a century of fishing companions, from my dad and my boyhood friends, through countless clients, to angling celebrities like Arnold and Ernie, I find that I'm drawn to a certain kind of person for fishing. I've been blessed with many good friends along the streams, and I'm grateful for all of them. But when I think of the ideal fishing companion now, I think first of Cal Dunbar, West Yellowstone businessman and for many years my favorite fishing buddy. Cal and I have fished together since the 1950s, and all those shared adventures and memories have a lot to do with how much fun we have today. We've gotten gradually better as fishermen, our hearing has gotten worse at about the same pace, and the same things make us laugh.

Cal comes to mind now partly because we just recently were featured on TBS's Montana segment of the "Portrait of America" series, fishing the Madison. It was a slow day, but Cal finally saved it by catching a beautiful brown trout on camera. This was in the summer of 1986, and in September I received a letter from Louise Vance, who produced the show, reporting on the film:

> This is just a note to let you know how very much we appreciated your letting us film with you. The footage looks *gorgeous*, and you and Cal make a great team. You have a lovely quality, and it comes through very clearly on film.

Well, I don't know about Cal, but nobody ever called *my* quality lovely before, so I figure it must have something to do with the two of us being together. Up until now I only thought it was lots of fun. Now I know it's even more than that.

*　　*　　*

There is much more to being an expert than having all the skills needed to catch fish, and being a good companion is very important. I would rather fish with someone who knows how to be a good fishing partner than with someone who knows the name of every insect in the river but who is rotten company.

Good companionship is difficult to define, partly because there are many different ways to have fun fishing and partly because people are different, depending upon what they're doing. I often am reminded of what my dad said about a man he knew: "He's a great guy to have a glass of beer with, but otherwise he's a son of a bitch."

For me it seems to start with enthusiasm. The person doesn't necessarily have to scream like crazy every time a fish is hooked, but it's good to know that someone is having fun with you and enjoying the whole experience.

The other important quality that I want in a fishing companion is noncompetitiveness. If I have to go with someone who counts all the fish he catches, and exaggerates how big they are, and wants to know just how many *I* caught and how big *they* were, I would rather not go.

I also enjoy all the talk. Fishing lets your mind be free, and it seems that the harder you concentrate on fishing, the more unusual are the thoughts that come into your head. So I guess I don't really want a silent partner.

I also like to be able to vary the pace. If I get tired, I want to be able to take a nap, or sit and watch the river, or be able to take it easy. Some fishermen aren't cut out to do that, so I suppose I want a companion who is open to that kind of variation. When you can do that, after a good day of fishing the cares of the world just don't seem to have as much weight.

That is a matter of not losing sight of an important rule: pace yourself. It's like the young bull and the old bull standing on the hill looking down at a bunch of heifers. The young bull says, "Let's run down the hill and get a couple of those heifers." And the old bull responds, "Let's *walk* down and get them all." When I was in college I worked for the street department in the city of Bozeman, and those people knew a lot about pace. The foreman saw me working one day and stopped me. "Wait a minute there! You're not gonna get done, so why hurry?" Fly fishing is like that. If you're doing it right, you're never really going to get done, so why hurry?

6

A TROUT'S
BEST FRIEND

Answering questions and minding business at the shop.

A brown trout, about twenty-two inches. We used to think nothing of killing a fish like this. Now we should think hard before we kill any at all.

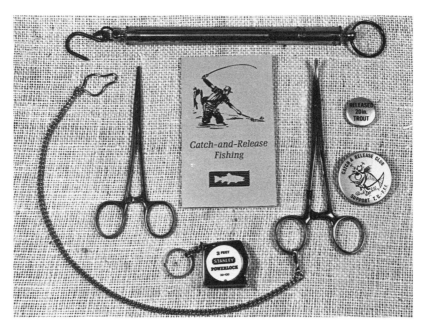

Our little promotion of the Catch-and-Release Club included the sale of items to make releasing fish easier, and an assortment of club pins.

Montana fishing is already great, but we can make it even
better. Photo by Montana Promotion Division,
Department of Commerce.

Back when Ma Wiedman and Buddy Lilly were taking a hundred fish a day from the Gallatin, nobody we knew thought much about the eventual effects of that kind of killing. There weren't that many of us fishing the streams, and we had a fairly simple idea of "waste." If we gave the fish to someone, or ate them ourselves, they weren't wasted. It took a long time for most of us to figure out that there is more than one way to waste a fish.

When I bought the Trout Shop I became owner of a big freezer that we used to store and freeze people's fish until they were ready to have them shipped home. Life was simple— you caught a big fish; you killed it. Only an idiot would let it go.

But gradually it dawned on me that we weren't going to be able to go on that way. As there were more and more fishermen, and as we learned about the ecology of a wild trout stream, we needed more good fishing at the same time that we learned that hatchery fish weren't a good answer. We were going to have to change our ways.

The change took many forms. During that 1960 winter that I spent in Arizona, I sat down and revised the old Martinez fishing map that we'd been handing out for so many years. I was getting uncomfortable with it because of the effects it had on the fishing. Don had put it together back when there were very few fishermen to read it, and he'd been very specific in it—park your car here, walk three hundred feet down the trail, turn left, cast behind the big rock—and now too many people were hitting too few spots too hard.

It was at that point that I decided that maps like Don's were creating fishermen who couldn't think for themselves, and that I realized that we needed to show them how. One of the best ways was to give them enough information so that they understood the river, tell them what kinds of flies were good, and send them to a general area with enough skill to find their own trout rather than sending them out to catch a fish that had Don's (or my) name on it.

I also did a lot of soul-searching about the Lunker Club,

and though I kept the book for fishermen until the late 1960s, I could see that it was on its way out, too. There again I saw that more fishermen meant more harvest, and the last thing I should be doing was encouraging people to kill fish and bring them in just to get their name in the book.

Of course, I didn't come to realize all these things on my own. Sportsmen went through a lot of changes in the 1960s, and fly fishermen more than most. A few farsighted anglers in Michigan created Trout Unlimited in 1959, and a couple years later Pat Halterman got Dan Bailey, me, and a few other well-known Montana fishermen together to form the Montana chapter of Trout Unlimited. Pat operated by administrative fiat; she just informed Dan and me that I was to be the president and he was to be the vice-president, and away we went. A few years later the Federation of Fly Fishermen (now the Federation of Fly Fishers) was created, and we began hearing about this organization back East, with people of Ed Zern's caliber as president, named Theodore Gordon Flyfishers. Their motto was "limit your kill, don't kill your limit." A few people, such as Lee Wulff, had been talking about this for a long time, but now it was a true movement, and it became clear that it was fishing's best hope. It also became clear that we weren't going to accomplish any of our goals easily.

We had to ensure the fish a safe place to swim; we had to protect their habitat if we expected them to reproduce and maintain wild trout populations. We had to regulate the fishing harvest so that those trout populations were not decimated. We had, in short, to overcome a lot of ingrained and traditional ideas about how the West should care for its natural resources.

The Trout Wars

That title does not overdramatize what happened. It may not often have been violent, but there were many violent emotions, and there was unlimited hostility. It's something for your soul to get up in front of a group of your neighbors and have them so angry with you that they're booing and hissing like you're a matinee villain. We went through that to drag

Montana fishing into the twentieth century.

Yellowstone Park was the pacesetter. Jack Anderson, who became superintendent of the Park in about 1967, was an avid fly fisherman and understood the harmful effects of hatchery trout and overharvest. There's a story that when he was superintendent of Grand Teton National Park in Wyoming, he forced the state of Wyoming to stop stocking Park streams; he told them that if they sent any of their hatchery people into the Park, his rangers would arrest them.

Under Jack's leadership, the Park Service in Yellowstone set an example with their special regulations. The superintendent has many exclusive powers because the Park was created before any of the surrounding states were even states, and Jack used that power well. In the early 1970s, catch-and-release regulations began to appear on Park waters, and they spread to several streams. At the same time, the U.S. Fish and Wildlife Service research project in the Park monitored the effects of the new regulations in order to see how they were working and if they needed revision. Yellowstone Lake regulations were fine tuned several times, resulting in a *maximum* size limit of thirteen inches, which protected the older age classes so important for spawning success. Writers all over the world have praised the fishing in the Park, and it really did help us to have that for an example.

But even then the managers in the states around the Park would look at the Park and say, "Yeah, but those are cut-throat trout. It's different with browns. These approaches won't work with other species." They also pointed out that though Jack Anderson may have had kingly powers to go out and do just what he thought was right, they didn't.

Of course there are lots of kinds of special regulations. The cutthroat is a different fish, but we weren't saying that we wanted Montana's trout managed exactly the way the Park managed its cutthroats. We were saying that through the use of various kinds of special regulations, Montana's trout could be managed a lot better than they were. And we were right, and have been proven right again and again, and I give the state a lot of credit for coming around, sometimes in the face of a lot of political resistance, and gradually increasing the amount of water regulated to improve the sport with no regard for angler harvest.

We went from the big-fish philosophy to the idea that we were going to have to share these fish with a lot more people. It wasn't that the quality of the fishing was going to decline, but that the chances of catching that big fish might be less because there was more competition for the fish. The number of big fish is probably greater on many waters now than it was thirty years ago. But there are more people after them.

The variety of special regulations we now have and with which we are experimenting did not come easily. Dick McGuire has to be credited with acknowledging that dumping hatchery trout in a healthy wild trout stream was a mistake. It took a lot of work and misery just to get the hatchery trout out of the rivers.

John Peters came to Montana from Michigan in the early 1960s as a project biologist for the state in Bozeman. John deserves a great deal of credit for teaching us that we must start by protecting the habitat. If you don't have a decent place for the trout to swim, there's no point in having them. The second part of the equation, once the habitat was secure, was keeping some trout in the water.

The state put Dick Vincent on the Madison to study the effects of hatchery trout on a wild trout population. He was one of the resisters. He still doesn't like the idea of restrictive regulations, but his study did prove that you harm the wild trout by putting hatchery trout on top of them.

Cal Dunbar, Charlie Brooks, and I formed a little club called the Southwestern Montana Fly Fishers in the early 1970s, and we used this organization and its letterhead as a vehicle to approach the problem.

We had to have a lot of hearings and bring in people to help. Ennis was really the seat of the problem on the Madison River. There was a group of sportsmen there addicted to hatchery trout. They were devoted to the old philosophy of bringing in the tourist, making sure he caught some fish by whatever means, and got to take some home, and they believed that that was the only way to have any tourism business. The resistance we faced in those meetings was immense, and I wasn't a very popular man in Ennis. The meetings got pretty hot, and once or twice I think the only thing that kept things peaceable was that Dick McGuire was big and could lick anybody in the place.

There was a lot of talk in Ennis about "our river," and "our valley," and why were people from West Yellowstone coming down and trying to screw up everything in Ennis. It was a terribly provincial attitude, the kind that would have gotten them in trouble in other ways eventually, because trout fishermen just can't afford to have only a local perspective anymore.

We had a meeting in the Silver Dollar Bar in Ennis one Sunday, and we invited all the opposition, sort of bearding them in their den. McGuire, who is about six feet six inches tall and weighs two hundred and twenty pounds, was running the meeting. Dick has not had the credit he deserves for getting the Madison River in the condition it is in today; he fought hard against the hatchery fish, and against the bullhead fishermen, and he did it all while he lived there. He faced those people every day, and it's hard to take on your friends and neighbors no matter how right you are. At this meeting in the bar, things got pretty rowdy, and people were starting to get up and threaten each other. Dick held a saltshaker in his fist and hammered it on the table a couple times. Everyone looked over, and he declared, "We're going to have to get this meeting back to *order*." Things were pretty quiet after that.

Of course it wasn't just a matter of convincing fishermen. The state Department of Fish, Wildlife and Parks had the same tendency to drag its feet. Like any political organization, it has a lot of people to keep happy. They moved very slowly until they saw that the pendulum was swinging the other way, and the evidence against hatchery fish and in favor of special regulations began to build up. There was a period there when the Trout Shop seemed to be singled out for some unusual attention by the game wardens. Of course, they could watch our guides as closely as they wanted, because we weren't breaking any laws, but it was an uneasy situation. We did have the feeling that the state was out for us for some time there.

Eventually the stream protection bill was passed, primarily through the efforts of John Peters. That protected the habitat through requiring certain instream flows at all times, and by keeping bulldozers and other equipment out of the streambed. A lot of states had laws like that for many years, but in Montana so much was wide open that this kind of change went against the grain. The new law also got rid of the hatchery trout in the Madison and allowed for the establishment of special regulations. This was not a narrowly defined term; it could mean catch-and-release, or a "slot limit" where certain sizes of fish had to be released. Fisheries managers have to be able to experiment with regulations to discover which ones will work best on which water. There are no simple "best rules" for all waters.

The best news, and the real proof that the fights were worthwhile, is that the fishing is getting better. The Madison trout fishing is improving in many parts of the river, and more recently, new regulations on the Yellowstone have shown great promise. I've noticed a big improvement — and it's being documented by the state — in the numbers and sizes of native cutthroat trout on the Yellowstone. That fishing is really getting better, in just three years since the regulations were put in effect. We can do it. We can have fishing like our parents and grandparents did here in Montana. The only difference is that we can't kill fish the way they did. I know that for some people fishing isn't worth it if they can't take some home to eat, and I suppose those people lose out in this situation. But we have to think of the future of the fish populations, and of the recreational industry, and of the young fishermen coming up, most of whom know nothing about the "good old days" when you could kill lots of fish and so won't miss that kind of fishing.

It's happening all over the state. Rock Creek, the Big

Hole, and other waters are responding to special regulations with fishing that will be spectacular in a few years. At the same time, it's become obvious that the new regulations have increased rather than decreased the amount of money out-of-state visitors will spend in areas like Ennis and West Yellowstone. The fishermen who can afford to travel long distances to have good fishing are mostly sportfishermen who aren't especially interested in fish as meat anyway. They just want to know that if they're going to come 2,000 miles to get to the fishing, there will be water good enough to support fish, and fish good enough to be worth catching.

What is disappointing is how slow people are to see the value of these changes. The Snake River in Wyoming could be a great trout fishery, but Wyoming is one of the most reluctant of western states to recognize the possibilities of new regulations. They could restore the area's badly tarnished reputation for sportfishing, generate a big influx in tourist revenue, and do justice to a really outstanding sport fish, the Snake River Cutthroat, but they are still locked in to the old ways of hatchery trout and kill-fisheries.

The Worth of a Trout

These are not easy times for Montana. The railroad, the ranchers, and the miners, who represent three of the state's biggest traditional business interests, are all having hard times. There is a story circulating in Montana about the rancher who won a million dollars in some lottery, and when someone asked him what he planned to do with the money, he said, "Well, I'm just going to keep on ranching until it's gone." Here in Montana, when you tell people that story, they laugh, but at the same time they nod their heads yes, because they recognize its truth. Because I care about the state that has been my family's home for more than a century, I've looked for ways to help. I think I've found some that will help not only the state's economic status but the state's trout as well.

We Montanans have been slow to recognize the economic asset that flows through our valleys. We too often have gotten hung up on some outdated sense of our "rights." We claim that "It's our right to catch and eat those trout," but we don't look beyond the good feeling it gives us to make that statement. It's not our right to do anything that may harm the state or its resources.

We can no longer think of our fish as part of a subsistence economy. Sure, you can claim that special regulations take food out of the mouths of your kids, but if your kids eat all the trout, they take food out of the mouths of the kids of a growing number of businessmen who are turning those trout into tourist dollars that are worth much more to all of us than the protein value of trout. The trout's highest value is not as food; it is worth much more on the recreational market than in the meat market.

Just recently I was guiding a pair of fly fishermen from out of state. I had agreed to give a day's guided fishing to anyone who donated $250 to the International Fly Fishing Center, and these two gentlemen had both done so. We were fishing the Yellowstone River a few miles downstream from Yankee Jim Canyon, and we were having a very good day. Both men had caught fish in the eighteen-inch range, and I felt like I'd given them the kind of day they would remember. While we were fishing along one bank, a man and a woman came drifting along the other bank in a rubber raft. The man was spin fishing, and he hooked a very big trout, probably weighing three or four pounds, which he finally beached on a long gravel bar across the river from us. One of my fishermen yelled over at him, "Let it go!" There was a little more hostility in the air than I would have liked, and the man yelled back, "I gotta eat, y' know!" and mashed this beautiful big brown trout over the head. As long as we keep thinking of our trout streams as our personal pantries, we're not going to do justice to them. Unlike our big game and our game birds, we have a choice when we fish for trout. There is no reasonable alternative for a hunter but to shoot the elk; there is a reasonable alternative for the trout fisherman, who can have all the pleasure of the stalk and the take without killing the game.

I had always promoted conservation in the Trout Shop catalog, but in 1974 I introduced our Catch-and-Release Club. When you joined you got a pin that said you were a member of the club, and then there were additional pins that said you'd released various sizes of trout up to twenty-four inches. You could either buy a set of pins or buy them individually. It was because of the Catch-and-Release Club that our shop got some wonderful attention from Arnold Gingrich. In his book, *The Joys of Trout*, he gave the club some recognition that was helpful in boosting it to national attention. His remarks sum up our philosophy so well that I quote them below.

CATCH AND RELEASE CLUB
Bud Lilly is a trout's best friend.
Fly-fishing's legion of honor decoration is the lapel recognition button devised by Bud Lilly, which reads "Released 20" Trout" and carries the slogan "Support F.F.F.–T.U." The club's purpose is to get fishermen familiar with the idea of releasing trout. Anybody can join. All that's needed is a dollar, and the simple statement that a trout of a certain size was returned to the water. The statement and the dollar can be sent to Bud Lilly, from November to May, Sourdough Road, Bozeman, Montana 59715, or to Bud Lilly, from May to November, in care of the Trout Shop, West Yellowstone, Montana 59587. Bud's pragmatic philosophy on keeping the membership requirement this simple reflects the belief that all fly fishermen are naturally honest and that any who are not will at least be publicizing the principle.
The principle of trout release, first and best stated by Lee Wulff, has since had many genial variations, one of the nicest of which is the Klamath Country Fly Caster's motto, "Keep your lines tight and your creels empty." But however it's codified it couldn't be better propagandized than by the general adoption and use of the Bud Lilly Catch and Release Club lapel buttons. Bud Lilly donates the proceeds from the sale of the release recognition buttons to Trout Unlimited and the Federation of Fly Fishers.

I quote that here not because it lets me show off how much attention the Trout Shop got, but because it reveals something about the attitudes of modern sportsmen, especially those who are willing to travel long distances to find good fishing for wild trout. Arnold, who was founding publisher of *Esquire* magazine, is typical of that group.

We have at least two choices in this issue. We can go on thinking of our local trout streams as the private larders of those of us who live nearby, or we can recognize what the rest of the world realized long ago, that these streams are a national treasure. I'm doing all I can to see to it that we take the latter course, and I'm doing it in ways that I am sure will benefit the state of Montana in the long run.

In 1976 a bunch of us—Dick McGuire, Ron Marcoux, Tom Morgan, Charlie Brooks, Dan Bailey, and others—got together and organized the Foundation for Montana Trout, a very specifically directed little institution whose purpose is to find ways to encourage the preservation of trout resources, especially but not exclusively in Montana. What we have done is raise enough money so that the interest from it can be used to fund worthy research projects related to wild trout management. It's a good cause, it's helping, and I recommend it to your attention as much as Trout Unlimited, the Federation of Fly Fishers, and the other organizations.

The Montana Ambassadors

The state of Montana, in order to develop its potential, has a program through which Governor Ted Schwinden has recently asked one hundred eighty citizens to act as "ambassadors." We start by contributing $150 each for this privilege, and the idea is that we can contact people we know, through our various business and personal connections, who might be interested in considering Montana a business opportunity. What I have concentrated on is a program we call the Ambassador Catch-and-Release Fly-Fishing Tour. We invite ten or twelve chief executive officers of potentially interested corporations to come out for a little fly-fishing adventure. We put them up on a nice guest ranch—we have used the Mountain Sky Guest Ranch in the Yellowstone Valley—and take them fishing, show them what the state's natural possibilities are, and give them some introduction to the economic possibilities as well. We started the program in 1985, based on a program that Nebraska developed around their wonderful bird shooting. The program is funded without state money, we insist on fly fishing and catch-and-release, and we expose some very influential people to the most current thinking in fishing management and ethics. At the same time, we subtly suggest by this example that we want them in Montana but we want to keep Montana's rare values at the same time.

The philosophy of this program was developed by John Wilson and Gary Buchanan of the state, both avid fly fishermen. It does have potential for conflict with other state departments, of course, as the state's Department of Fish, Wildlife and Parks has a more broad approach to managing most of the state's fisheries than just fly fishing. But so far it's working, and I don't mind increasing the chances that incoming executives with political power will already be converted to fly fishing.

There is no way that Montana can continue relying on the timber industry, and mining, and even agriculture to the extent it used to. I'd like to see my kids have a chance to live here without the risk of having to move to Sunnyvale, California. And we are now in a position to direct the state so that the values that matter to so many people, including such things as healthy trout streams, can be protected.

The Greater Yellowstone Coalition

In 1986 it was my pleasure to be named to the board of the Greater Yellowstone Coalition. This is an umbrella organization of dozens of local, regional, and national organizations, all of which have some interest in seeing to it that the important values of the Yellowstone area are protected. Greater Yellowstone includes more than ten million acres, at the heart of which is Yellowstone Park, but which also includes the several surrounding national forests and a great amount of state and private land as well. The idea that this area should have some kind of unified management plan, or at least some clearly understood general management direction, is an old one, but only in the last few years have the area's friends joined together to try to influence the many federal, state, and local agencies, as well as the private landowners, to look at the bigger picture rather than try to manage the area piecemeal. The piecemeal approach, which had each forest supervisor, town manager, park ranger, homeowner, and businessman saying, "What I do is my own business," was destructive, and in the long run it was reducing the area's unique values. The grizzly bear is often used as an example of why the area's management needs to be coordinated; it is a far-ranging wild animal that knows nothing about jurisdictions and boundaries. But the bear is only a small part of the issue, which involves all the elements of this setting, including some of the best, wildest watersheds in the country.

I am promoting the notion that the watersheds of this uniquely endowed region are in fact the best barometer of its health. They interconnect it all, and no manager can afford to act without concern for other managers both upstream and downstream. The ecosystem's network of aquatic resources demand much of our attention if we are going to care for the land they drain.

I visualize a stronger system of interagency communication (just as now exists in fire management, or bear management, or elk management) between fisheries managers throughout the Greater Yellowstone area. There is far too little consistency in fishery management in this great region.

For example, the brown trout that migrate in the fall out of Hebgen Lake up the Madison River must migrate through a short stretch of water between the lake and Yellowstone Park before they can reach their spawning areas. The regulations in that short piece of water are far too liberal and allow the shortstopping of a significant part of the run. I object to that because it reduces the sport of the no-kill fishermen, who these days are the ones contributing the most to the local economy. I object to it also for esthetic reasons; that spawning run is an exciting natural event, and in an area known for its natural wonders, we ought to interfere a little less than that. It's like the steelhead having to run through a maze of gill nets on Pacific Coast rivers. We have to think about what's really most important for us here. We can keep many of the traditional practices, but we have to reconsider them all to make sure we're keeping the right ones.

I know that we can't manage all parts of the West with the same level of control and preservation as we can manage the Greater Yellowstone ecosystem. I also know that even in the Yellowstone area we would be foolish to try to stop growth and change; we live here, and we need many things the land can give us. But I am sure that with areas like Greater Yellowstone as models, we can do a much better job than we have almost everywhere. Nobody is asking for perfection. What we're after is improvement. And there are few better ways to measure improvement than by the number of miles of healthy trout stream an area has.

The Future of Montana's Fishing

I hope to see more and more waters in the West regulated in a way that will allow the fish population to remain robust while providing a lot of sport. That may mean catch-and-release, or it may mean some other form of special regulations, but it will usually mean the elimination of bait fishing, which simply kills too many fish to be permitted in a wild trout fishery. The many studies that have been done prove beyond a doubt that you will lose more than fifty percent of all fish hooked on bait and then released, while you will lose less than ten percent of those hooked and released on lures that have only one hook or group of hooks, or on flies.

The big thrill for the modern angler is catching, not eating. It's like golf: you don't have to eat the balls to have fun. I know that many people still enjoy killing and eating trout, and there is nothing wrong with that in moderation. Many of our streams will probably always be able to sustain a certain harvest. I also know that bait fishing is one of the longest established sporting traditions in this country, and that there are some people for whom it is the only way to fish. We will always have to have some bait fishing. But times must change. There were times when bear baiting, set guns, punt guns, and all sorts of other practices that we now regard as bad were perfectly acceptable. I'm proud of my education as a Montana sportsman, which started out with bait fishing as much as it did with fly fishing. But I learned that it is no longer possible to fish the way I did fifty or even thirty years ago. I used to kill as many fish as any other fisherman, probably more sometimes because I was pretty good at catching them. I hardly ever kill one any more, because I know that the fishing experience is in greater demand now, and we have to share this resource among a growing number of people.

It looks to me as if here in Montana more and more people are switching to fly fishing. The ranks of the bait fishermen are being thinned. There are still plenty of places where bait fishing is popular, and there is comparatively little water even now where bait fishing is prohibited. Bait fishermen do not yet have much to complain about.

But I'm not sure I believe that bait fishing is essential in modern sport fishing. I've heard all the traditional arguments like, "Here's old Joe, he's eighty, and he can't get around," or, "Here's little Johnny, he's only four," and these people have to fish with bait. If the fishing is well managed so that there are plenty of fish, those same people can take fish on artificial lures. Spinning rods and fly rods don't cost any more than casting rods, and anyone with even a little coordination, such as almost all eighty-year-olds and four-year-olds certainly have, can learn to cast those outfits. "Well," they say, "old Joe just wants to sit there with his line in the water. You can't do that with flies or spoons or spinners." And that's true, but I don't think that old Joe has to worry for a long time about not finding a place to do that. If I were pushed to the wire, I guess I'd say let's keep some places where old Joe can bait fish. Even Yellowstone Park has reserved some streams for kids to bait fish. But if we manage the water correctly, we can greatly reduce the need for that kind of fishing by making good fishing so common that fewer and fewer people will even want to use bait.

But let's be honest about this. Those very old and very young fishermen are always trotted out to defend bait fishing, but the people doing the justifying are healthy, adult fishermen who are really just using those small, special groups to defend their own preference for bait fishing. Even if we have to take care of the needs of some special groups, that doesn't justify bait fishing by the rest of the people. We can find good fishing places for old Joe, and we can teach little Johnny how to spin fish or fly fish by the time he's six or seven. We shouldn't confuse our desire to protect the needs of these special cases with our greater need to maintain good sport fisheries, and we shouldn't sacrifice the opportunities to develop those good sport fisheries out of some misplaced sense of loyalty to a tiny minority of the fishermen who may need special attention.

Besides an increase in special regulations, there are two other areas that I see getting additional management attention in Montana's future. The first is lake fishing. Managers are taking lakes more seriously. Flathead Lake, for example, has been polluted with all kinds of fish. So many lakes are managed as if they're big holding tanks where the state dumps in fish one day and people yank them out the next. Lakes can be managed by the same kinds of ecological principles as rivers, and they can produce fabulous fisheries. Many will never support natural populations of fish, but many others can. We have a long way to go in Montana before we really are doing justice to our lakes.

The other area getting more management attention is spring creeks. Montana has a fabulous collection of spring creeks, more than seventy of them, and according to a recent report by the American Fisheries Society in cooperation with the state of Montana, almost all of them are in degraded condition. There is no excuse for this. Again, the most compelling argument is probably the economic one. Spring-creek

fishing is a treasured experience among anglers all over the
world, and it is hard to come by. Montana may have more of
these creeks than any other state, and it has a great opportunity to benefit fisheries while generating an influx of tourist
dollars. There are many directions to be explored, including
conservation easements for landowners, state purchase of
fishing rights or outright purchase of property, tax incentives
for stream restoration, and so on. All we need to do is
recognize the values, both esthetic and economic, of these
marvelous little aquatic ecosystems.

Getting to the Fishing Once We Have It

Access is a growing problem. Things are going to get more
crowded, and so it's going to be more important that we take
care of every mile of fishable stream. The Clark's Fork is
being cleaned up. I foresee a day in the future when the Yellowstone River will be a good trout fishery as far downstream
as Billings. It's good now as far as Big Timber, which hasn't
always been true. Like the spring creeks, Montana's big rivers
give us an opportunity few other states have. We can actually
increase the number of miles of good fishing rivers, and we
are doing it right now.

But still we will have a growing access problem, and
recent court battles over access have introduced a lot of hard
feelings. I hope that the day comes when we consider some
arrangement of tax incentives or even supplemental payments
to encourage people to permit public fishing on their property.

This is a challenging problem, and it is going to get more
challenging. We have been through a period of considerable
animosity between sportsmen and landowners, and until we get
into a more communicative and cooperative mood, access
issues are going to make more headlines than progress.

One answer, or partial answer, that I am pursuing actively
is the purchase of good fishing, either by government agencies,
or by organizations, or by private individuals. All of these
approaches have been tried with some success in Montana and
in other states, but there is much more that can be done.

Through my Western Rivers Club, and through my wife's real estate connections, we are attempting to get the right lands into the right hands. It won't solve all the problems, but it is a part of the process we must go through in Montana to get our good fishing sorted out.

I was visiting a ranch in the Madison Valley recently, talking to the old-timer who owned the place. I noticed a small stream meandering across a brush field. When I asked the owner about it, he told me it was a spring creek. Of course, the discovery of a new spring creek is always exciting, so I asked the rancher about it.

"Jack, are there any fish in that little creek?"

"Oh, yeah, there were a bunch of brook trout in it. We finally got rid of 'em. Had a hell of a time getting them out of there." Brook trout were so unimportant to these people that they actually poisoned them, as if they were rats.

Jack and his family are good people, working a ranch that is losing money badly. He knows nothing about fishing or its potential in the economic future of today's West. He knows ranching, and cattle, and a way of life that is tragically disappearing. We all should mourn its passing, for it produced strong and self-reliant people who made Montana a great state in which to live. But it *is* passing, and we have a chance to replace it with things that will keep Montana a great place in which to live. Those things include a system of rivers and lakes that are getting the respect they deserve, and are giving back to us the pleasure and fulfillment we need.

7

ONCE A GUIDE

Fish stories in front of the Trout Shop.

Mel Kreiger and Esther Lilly conclave at West Yellowstone.

When Pat and I retired, we decided we wanted to keep in touch with the many friends we had made at the Trout Shop. So we developed our Western Rivers Club. The purpose of the club was to provide members (who paid fifty dollars to join) with a variety of informational services to help them prepare for fishing trips to our part of the West. We had spent thirty years accumulating knowledge about the fishing, and we still had many contacts that helped us keep up-to-date on fishing conditions. Retirement allowed us the time to explore more of the fishing ourselves, and the club was the best way we knew to put all that to use while continuing to enjoy all the friendships.

We applied to it the same principle we had applied to the Trout Shop. We emphasized that western fishing was more than just fishing, it was a "total experience" that had all manner of things to offer. Each newsletter would have information on recent books and publications about the West, including historical material and natural history. There were frequent reports from us about lodges and restaurants we had checked out, as well as the usual information about fishing conditions. If some interesting piece of information came out on a topic we thought would be of interest to members, we'd just mail it off by itself. We very quickly were developing a fine network of information sources, and the members seemed to appreciate it. They could call us up for trip planning before they came, or they could call us up if they were already out here fishing and were having a hard time finding what they wanted.

Pat had always had a premonition that she would die young. When she was sixteen she suffered from rheumatic fever and was actually given last rites two or three times. Her mother was always pessimistic about Pat's health after that, and she convinced Pat that she was going to die before her time.

Pat smoked heavily, and during the last few years of her life she was suffering from respiratory problems, including emphysema. Her health had a lot to do with our getting out of the business when we did. In January of 1981 she became very ill with pneumonia, and while she was hospitalized, some X rays revealed a spot on her lung that eventually was diagnosed as lung cancer. An operation was apparently successful in removing it in February of 1983, but her lungs were in such bad shape that removing the whole lung couldn't be risked. In August of that year they discovered a spot on the other lung, and the doctor told her she didn't have much time. She went through a good deal of suffering as heroically as anyone could, though what with radiation treatments and all the other aspects of fighting the disease, it was a very rough time. She passed away on April 14, 1984.

Anyone who has been happily married knows what a shocking loss such a death is, even if you think you're prepared for it. We had thirty-seven wonderful years together. We raised a family anyone would be proud of, and we did it in the beautiful country we all loved so much. She was laid to rest in a small cemetery outside Manhattan, Montana, where a spring creek flows along the edge of the gravesites. The loss of Pat was very painful for all of us. She had been the family's directing spirit just as she had been the manager of the Trout Shop, and we all agreed that the epitaph on her stone should read simply, "Our Strength."

At that point I decided to discontinue the Western Rivers Club, so I sent out a last newsletter telling the members that I was shutting it down but would continue to keep in touch with all of them periodically. I did that, sending out an occasional item of interest, such as some important announcement on the Greater Yellowstone Coalition, for example. Just recently I have decided that the time is right, for me and for fishermen, to reactivate the Club, and as I write this it's already back in full swing. If you're interested, contact me at 2007 Sourdough Road, Bozeman, Montana 59715. We're having a lot of fun with the Club. Once a guide, always a guide.

* * *

Early in 1984 Pete Van Gytenbeek, then president of the Federation of Fly Fishers, called me and asked if I would take on the chairmanship of the International Fly Fishing Center in West Yellowstone. After some false starts and bad luck with fundraising, the FFF had arranged to lease the old Union Pacific dining hall building, known locally as the Convention Center, as the home of the IFFC, but there was a world of work to be done in getting it into shape and developing a program that would make it the functional and important institution it could become. I wasn't too enthusiastic, but Pat encouraged me, pointing out that soon I was going to be alone and I would need a project of this size to keep me occupied and productive.

Working with Esther Simon, executive director of the Federation, I was able to get the IFFC off the ground, and we had a grand dedication ceremony at the Conclave in August of 1984, with Montana Governor Ted Schwinden and several other regional dignitaries attending. The best thing that came out of it for me, looking back, was working with Esther. I needed someone with her energy and commitment to keep me encouraged in what was a very rough time for me, and Esther made sure I saw what needed to be done, knowing that if I saw it I'd find a way to do it. Out of that professional friendship and working together eventually came a deeper attachment, and in October of 1985 Esther and I were married. She now is working in real estate in Bozeman, and I find myself with a whole new family consisting of Esther and her two young children from a previous marriage, Alisa and Christopher.

Esther's encouragement has continued to be important to me. I needed someone to keep me active and in gear, doing things that were important to me but that I might not have done left on my own. I was lucky to be able to retire young, and there are many things I enjoy doing. Being an ardent conservationist who has worked for several important organizations, she encouraged me to get involved with various good causes, such as my work with the Greater Yellowstone Coalition and the Montana Ambassadors, and her encouragement had a lot to do with me getting around to writing the books that people have been after me to write for so many years. She shares my love of rivers and the West, and though it's quite a challenge being a daddy again, we've built a new life that's very exciting. I've been donating quite a few fishing trips to the International Fly Fishing Center and the Greater Yellowstone Coalition, so many that I think I may cut back and do a little more fishing for myself. Even guides like a day to themselves now and then.

*   *   *

I finally went to Alaska in 1982, the first summer after I sold the shop. I fished the rivers flowing into Bristol Bay, and I found that a lot of the fishing was so easy that it was possible to lose interest. When you can catch thirty or forty silver salmon weighing eight to fifteen pounds each in one day, you get jaded pretty quickly. They are tremendous fish, great jumpers, and Alaska simply must be preserved so that experiences like that can always be had, but I discovered that I wouldn't want what it has to offer on a daily basis.

We were fishing the Alagnak, moving up and down it by boat, and my favorite fishing was for rainbows and grayling. The rainbows were a little larger on the average than those in the Madison, fourteen to twenty inches. It was especially nice because we fished only that one river, which had everything we could have wanted, and spent no time flying around in helicopters and airplanes. I caught silver salmon, king salmon, pike, grayling, and rainbows, and after a week I was ready to come home. The rough, wild country was itself worth the trip, though — the bears were all over the place, we had ptarmigan walking through camp, and so on — and I enjoyed all the things I dreamed of as a child, including some wonderful streamside salmon dinners cooked over open fires. Everyone who loves fly fishing in primitive settings should fish Alaska.

Seeing Alaska now, with all its fabulous fishing and wild country, was worth it to me for another reason. Forty years ago I had been ready to go up there and be a guide and live what I thought would be a great, romantic life. Now I'm glad

I did what I did. I don't think I would have stuck if I'd gone there then, partly because there was comparatively little fly-fishing guiding going on back then and partly because the challenge of the fishing is not suited to my temperament. We all think we'd just love easy fishing for huge fish until we get it, then it pales more quickly than we could have imagined.

So I'm here, surrounded by Montana's great country with its mountains and wildlife and trout streams. I have more family and friends than a man has any right to hope for, and I have a lot to do. Esther and I are planning some fishing trips to countries we've always dreamed of — New Zealand, Chile, and so on — and I'd like to go back to Alaska and catch some more of those rainbows. And of course there's all the fishing close to home.

And I remember a day on the Madison during the salmon-fly hatch, years ago. I was fishing with a good friend, Sam Radan, and we'd already caught some big trout, when just downstream from Varney Bridge I saw a fish rising to the naturals in midstream. I worked my way out to him, right up to the top of my chest waders, and confidently put a fly over him. No take. I moved closer and tried again. I tried different flies, different tippets. I moved closer. I could see that he weighed four or five pounds; he was throwing spray like another fish weighing over five pounds which I'd caught earlier that day. I got so close he was actually throwing spray on my glasses when he rose. Sam was watching from the bank. I'd cast, the fish would rise and take a natural, Sam would cuss, and I'd cast again. Nothing worked.

I didn't catch him. He never stopped rising, and I never spooked him, but he just wouldn't take. It may be something you didn't think you needed to learn to do, but it's a humbling part of your education as a fly fisherman to have to walk away from an eagerly rising trophy trout just because you can't catch him. There are lots of fish out there that I haven't caught yet, and there are some that I'll probably have to walk away from. I'm looking forward to all of it.